THE

Afterlife

I went to Eternity in Heaven

What occurs in the Afterlife,
Heaven, the Millennium, and Eternity?

DEBBIE CARTER

Studio of Books LLC
5900 Balcones Drive Suite 100
Austin, Texas 78731
www.studioofbooks.org
Hotline: (254) 800-1183

Ordering Information:
Special discounts are available on quantity purchases by corporations, associations, and others. For details, contact the publisher at the address above.

Printed in the United States of America.

ISBN-13:   Softcover   979-8-9900465-3-5
           eBook   978-1-964148-99-1

Library of Congress Control Number: 2024905877

CONTENTS

Chapter Nine

Chapter Ten

Chapter Eleven

Chapter Twelve

INTRODUCTION

I went into anaphylactic shock and momentarily died. My angel came for me and took me to Eternity in Heaven. I stood by God in His Shekinah Glory, and He showed me the Holy City, New Jerusalem. I saw the beautiful layers of color in the walls, on the doors, and the cornerstones. God told me to seal up my experience because His people were not yet ready to hear about Eternity. That was thirty-five years ago.

Later, I was encouraged to do an in-depth study of the Book of Revelation. I then taught it for five years. During this time of teaching was the first time in twenty-five years that I spoke openly about seeing New Jerusalem and my experience in Eternity.

I now enjoy teaching what the Bible tells us about the Afterlife. My desire is for you to understand the Rapture, Heaven, the Millennium, and our Eternity. I will give scriptural information about our future and explain many events that are going to take place in the Afterlife. I write with simplicity and in an easy-to-understand context with explanations.
I want the new, and the mature believers to have a greater depth of understanding of our life to come. I pray for you to be encouraged, and for your life to be enriched.

Debbie Carter has written a masterful resource for those desiring greater knowledge and insight into end-time events and the afterlife. Her in-depth exploration of God's truths found in Scripture, along with her own personal revelatory experience, will certainly encourage readers in their hope of Christ's return and the wonders to come in the eternal future!

Pastor Brent Mitchell
Pastor of Pastoral Care,
Trinity Fellowship Church
Amarillo, Texas

Chapter One

◇◇◇◇

ANAPHYLACTIC SHOCK

I WENT IN for my yearly doctor's appointment, and the doctor said he felt a possible tumor. I was scheduled to have two tests done, a sonogram and a barium enema x-ray. They were standard tests that would take less than an hour.

On Friday, February 6, 1987, two days after the doctor's appointment, I went in at 9:00 a.m. to the lower level of the hospital to have the two procedures done. The first test was the sonogram. A sonogram is a computer picture of areas inside the body created by high-energy sound waves. It went well, and later confirmed that I did not have a tumor.

After the sonogram, I went to another room for the barium enema x-ray. A barium enema is an x-ray that takes pictures of the colon, while an enema tube inserted in the rectum delivers the liquid barium. It detects changes or abnormalities in the large intestine and makes the lower intestinal tract visible on an x-ray film.

For the first part of the barium x-ray, I laid on my back, and the doctor inserted the tip of the tube and started the liquid barium flow. Within a few minutes, my eyes began to itch, and I thought I had gotten something in them. Within another minute, my eyes were burning, and my lips were tingling. I asked the doctor how long this procedure would take, and he said about ten minutes. They turned me over onto my stomach to continue the x-ray. My face and neck were now feeling flushed. I asked the nurse if the barium would cause me to feel flushed and become hot, and much to my surprise, she said no. It was at this point that I knew something was wrong.

My eyes continued to itch. My lips were tingling and starting to swell, and my stomach was beginning to hurt. I started pleading the blood of Jesus over my body and repeating Philippians 4:13. "I can do all things through Christ Who strengthens me." Again and again, I prayed to my Heavenly Father, and I said to myself, "I can get through a few more minutes." By the time the ten-minute x-ray was over, and I could get off the table, I was weak, shaky, and unstable, but I managed to get to the dressing room.

I looked in the mirror in the dressing room, and it was hard to recognize myself. My face was red and my eyes and lips were swollen. I opened the dressing room door into the larger room, stumbled out and sat down on a chair. I bent over with my elbows on my knees and my face in my hands. I told the nurse I was sick to my stomach, and she said she would get me a pan to throw up in. I said, "No, I am not that kind of sick." I was starting to have trouble breathing. Then, I fell off the stool to the floor onto my hands and knees. I remember hearing the word stretcher before I passed out. I later learned I had gone into anaphylactic shock.

Anaphylactic shock is also known as anaphylaxis. It is a sudden, severe, and life-threatening allergic reaction to something. The reaction affects the whole body and involves the respiratory and cardiovascular systems. The itching of the eyes and a hot, flushed face with swelling of the tongue and lips, and the constricting of the airways marks anaphylaxis.

The blood pressure drops, and the pulse becomes weak yet rapid, causing a collapse, or loss of consciousness. It may also include abdominal pain, cramps, nausea and vomiting, a skin rash, hives, and swelling that can be beneath the skin and on the surface. It usually reaches its peak severity within five to thirty minutes. Anaphylaxis requires immediate medical attention and, if left untreated, can get worse quickly and lead to unconsciousness and death within fifteen to thirty minutes.

The difference between an allergic reaction and anaphylaxis is that people who have an allergic reaction often have skin symptoms such as a rash and swelling of the face, lips, and eyes. Anaphylaxis involves the respiratory and cardiovascular systems.

Anaphylaxis is the most dangerous of all allergic reactions because it involves more than one body system. Anaphylaxis requires an injection of epinephrine that rapidly reverses the anaphylactic symptoms. Common triggers of anaphylaxis include certain foods, some medications, perfumes, insect venom, and latex.

After I collapsed on the floor, the next thing I remember is lying on my back on a table with several nurses around me. An IV of epinephrine was being put in my left arm. Epinephrine is an adrenaline, it is a hor*mone* and neurotransmitter used to restore cardiac rhythm and controls congestion. I was struggling to breathe. I was hot, my eyes, face, lips, and tongue were swollen, and I had pains and cramps in my abdomen. The nurse repeatedly took my blood pressure and reported the numbers. I was thirty-eight years old, and I had no reason to know or have paid attention to blood pressure numbers up to this point. I did not understand what blood pressure numbers meant or why they kept repeating them.

I was a born-again, spirit-filled Christian believer in Jesus for only two years. I had read a book about the power of the blood of Jesus, and I understood a few things about God's protection over me. I started claiming the blood of Jesus over my body, along with His covering and His protection. A nurse kept repeating my blood pressure numbers, and I prayed. "God, if I only knew what the blood pressure numbers meant, I would know if I was going to live or die."

I was shaking, trembling, pulling my legs and knees up, and laying them back on the table. The cramping and pain in my abdomen came and went like labor contractions. Even though I was going in and out of consciousness, I could hear the nurses talking, and I knew what was going on around me most of the time. I heard the nurse say that the rest of my body was swelling and that I was breaking out in hives, even on the palms of my hands. I was hot, but I was cold, and they were getting a warm blanket to put on me. I remember saying out loud, the best I could, to please call my husband at our home. They were putting more medicine in my IV, and the nurses were bustling around me. I remember praying, "God, you have brought me too far for something like this to happen."

It was then that things began to change. I felt something warm touch my right arm. I opened my swollen eyes and saw my angel standing there.

I knew immediately that he was my angel. It is not something you will be mistaken about if you see your angel. You will know in your spirit.

He laid his hand gently on my right arm, covering my arm between my elbow to my wrist. His hand was so large it covered my whole arm. Oh, how warm his hand was, so soft and gentle! He was big and beautiful. He must have been about seven feet tall, and I knew this because he was much taller than anyone else that had stood beside me. He was bright and outlined with a radiant white glow all around him. I could not see his facial features because his face was filled with white glowing light. He was wearing a white garment that went over his head. It did not have a collar, but I could see his garment had a slight opening at his neck on his chest. The sleeve of his garment was wider and fuller at the sleeve's opening, where his hand stretched out on my arm. I remember thinking, "Angel," and then totally relaxing. I felt my legs relax as I laid them flat on the table. My stomach quit aching, and I felt my arms and whole body fully relax.

I then felt my soul rise out of my earthly body and move above my earthly body on the table. I could feel the space between my two bodies. My angel took me, and we ascended to the room's ceiling. I looked down and could see both bodies. I saw my earthly body on the table, and I saw my raised body about two feet above my earthly body. Both bodies were identical, both were laid out flat, horizontally. The raised body was fully clothed, but it was transparent, and I could see through it, seeing both bodies at the same time.

It was many years later before I realized I had described three of myself in the room that day. The body on the table, the second was the raised body, and the third was when I saw all of this from the ceiling with my angel. We are made up of body, soul, and spirit. The body on the table was my earthly body, the body raised was my soul, and what I saw and described from the ceiling was my spirit. It is our spirit that communicates with God, so it was my spirit that went to Eternity.

I moved from being with my angel at the ceiling, looking down upon the room, to being upright in Eternity. It was, and still is, very hard to describe what I saw and felt. I have searched for words to express my time in Eternity, but describing feelings, emotions, atmosphere, distance, and colors is quite challenging. The colors, the softness, the air around me, and the quietness are difficult to describe in earthly terms. How could

I feel softness around me, but I did. There was a soft, white, airy, and transparent flow around me. There was an ultimate quietness, silence, and calmness that I had never known or felt before. It was all-encompassing, and peace was everywhere.

Though it is hard to explain, I was both standing and suspended in the air. I looked down and saw my feet. A little more coverage of this soft white substance, like a cloud, was slightly moving over and around my feet and ankles. Then, I looked at the palms of my hands. I never found a reason, nor has it been revealed, why I was looking at my feet and the palms of my hands, but I was. My arms were at my side with my forearms stretched out from my side with the palms of my hands turned up.

I looked up abruptly, sensing, knowing there was a presence to my right. Next to me was a huge bright, significant area like a thick cloud. It was so bright! In my spirit, I knew that I was in God's presence. This shape was a big beautiful bright cloud much more extensive and denser than anywhere else. It was overwhelming. I would later understand this to be God in His Shekinah Glory. Shekinah is a Hebrew word meaning *dwelling* and denotes the divine presence of God. I was seeing God's Shekinah Glory.

I did not see God. I could not see Him, and I knew I would not see Him. I knew this in my spirit. But His presence was there, and it was very strong. I was in the presence and glory of God, in the beauty of His spirit. I knew it, and He was communicating with me in my spirit. There were no words spoken as the communication was all within my spirit. I was bathed in the glory of God all around me.

Instantly, I understood that He knew everything about me. Everything I had ever said or done was captured in the unexplainable knowledge that God knew me. He knew about my whole life all at once, my entire life in one second. I felt an overwhelming love, acceptance, and freedom that I had never known or felt before. I knew I was truly loved and accepted by Him just as I was, right then, right there by Him. I was aware that I was standing in His presence, and His glory was all around me. I was in mid-air, standing by His Shekinah Glory cloud. I was peaceful and quiet on the outside, but I cannot describe the intense excitement inside of me. I do not know the words to describe what I felt inside. Even as I write this, my heart is pounding, and my hands and arms tingle, and I can see all of it, feel all I felt in His presence.

No one can never, ever talk me out of where I was and what I saw in Eternity. With God as my witness, I was in Eternity and in God's presence. I was standing next to God's glory cloud when something caught my attention. I looked up, and straight ahead, I was looking at something enormous and beautiful floating at a distance in front of me. I knew immediately that I was seeing the New Jerusalem in Eternity. I knew where I was and what I was seeing. It did not need to be explained to me. Amazingly, I had no hesitation or question about it. God revealed these things to me in my spirit, and I understood. I was seeing New Jerusalem with its beautiful, brilliant, and bright colors suspended in the air in front of me.

One moment I was next to God's Shekinah Glory, and then, without knowing or feeling anything, I had moved much closer to New Jerusalem. I was not next to God's Shekinah Glory anymore, but I could still feel God's presence beside me. New Jerusalem was so much closer, and now the details were very visible.

I could see two walls and three cornerstones. I was looking at a long wall with a cornerstone on the left and a cornerstone on the right. I could see another wall that was connected to the right cornerstone that went far away from me into the distance connecting to the third cornerstone. God revealed to me that the wall down the right side was the east wall.

There were three arched doors on the front wall and three arched doors down the side of the east wall. Each door had a half-circle shape at the top of the door. The doors were massive and evenly spaced in the walls, and the doors were closed. The arched doors were a solid light khaki or light tan in color. The doors went up about one-third of the giant wall.

From the foundation base of the walls, going up were brilliant layers of colors. They were magnificent shades of bright greens, blues, purples, yellows, and reds, each having its own layer of brilliant color. The layers of colors were bright and shone like a crystal glass of color. There was a significant layer of color on top of another layer of color until they reached the top of the doors and stopped where the arch of the door started.

A bright light shone through the colored layers from the inside of the wall. This light coming through the colors gave the layers the appearance of brilliant crystal glass. I cannot say which color came first or second, just that there were layers of color and what colors I saw. The best I can describe the colors in earthly terms would be seeing a very large multi-colored stained-glass window in a church. With the bright morning sun shining through the stained glass and looking at the bright blues, reds, greens, purples, and yellows, seeing the distinct individual crystal colors. It is not easy to describe something God makes compared to the earthly things that man makes.

As I said, the layers of colors did not go all the way to the top of the wall. The colors stopped where the half-circle arch began on the doors. The layers of colors somehow overlapped at each color's edge, but the layers of color did not make blended colors. Where the horizontal layers of colors connected on top of one another, the colors were soft and not abrupt. The layers of color went across the front of the wall. The colors and doors both sat on the foundation floor of the wall.

From the left cornerstone were the layers of color, then a door, the same layer of colors, and the second door, the same colors, and the third door with the colors ending at the right cornerstone. This same pattern of layers of color and the three closed doors continued down the east wall that went far in the distance.

Above the layers of bright colors were two-thirds of the rest of the wall to the top. The two-thirds of the wall above the layers of color were various shades of tan. Starting above the layers of color was a tan color, gradually going to a lighter tan until it reached the top of the wall. The tan color of the wall changed so gradually that I barely noticed the change in color. The wall was also a different tan than the solid light khaki tan color of the doors. On top of the tall wall was a flat ledge. The ledge was an even lighter, whiter shade of color than the wall.

The cornerstones were completely different from the walls. The cornerstones were square, more significant, heavier, thicker, and taller than the walls. They consisted of large rough irregular stones in the shape of squares and rectangles. They were colored in slightly different shades of light tans.

There was a capstone that finished off the top of each of the towering cornerstones. The square capstone was a little higher in the middle but not very tall, going down to each corner and forming a square sitting on top of each cornerstone. The color of the capstones was the same color as the ledge on top of the wall. The capstone and the ledge were the same color and the lightest of all the colors. The height of the wall came up to where the capstone started, then by adding the capstone, the cornerstones were taller than the walls.

Another beautiful amazing thing I saw was the bright multi-colored layers in the wall reflecting on the lower part of the left cornerstone. The reflection of the colors on the cornerstone was spectacular. The bright colors did not reflect on the doors or the right cornerstone. This was amazing!

I am using the descriptive word "clouds" because that is the best word, I know to help visualize what I saw. There were differences in the cloud's shapes, sizes, denseness, and flow.

1. There was the huge, very bright white dense Shekinah Glory cloud of God.
2. The movement of the light soft cloud that was around my feet and ankles.
3. The space between the New Jerusalem and me had very few clouds and movement, but the clouds were still visible to me.

Inside the walls

I knew the city of New Jerusalem was inside the beautiful walls. However, I did not see any part of the city itself. What I did see was a cream-colored white, massive, enormous mountain cloud that filled the inside of the walls where the city was. It was like a beautiful fluffy cloud, soft, creamy, white, and somewhat moving as a cloud does. It was not as bright or as dense as God's Shekinah cloud but was still very bright. The big mountain shape was very tall, many times the height of the walls. This explained why I could *only see* the front and east walls. This beautiful mountain cloud inside the walls hid the back and left walls and the fourth cornerstone. I knew it was the glory of God that filled the inside of the walls, and this light was illuminating through the bright colors in the walls. I knew in my spirit where I was and what I was seeing, New Jerusalem in Eternity. I was in Eternity, the believer's eternal home. The New Jerusalem was there in the air, with the glory of God inside. I knew what I was seeing, even though

I had never seen anything like it before. I was in God's glory, suspended in air and time, and looking at God's beautiful walls and His glorious mountain, the city of New Jerusalem.

When the spirit revealed all at once the whole picture to me of where I was and Who I was with, I suddenly stopped. I was not ready to be in Eternity. I was not prepared to leave my family. I felt like I was speaking for the first time. "Oh God, not yet, I still have children!"

It was much later in life that I realized God had no intention of me staying in Eternity. He was showing it to me, that explained to me why the doors were closed.

In an instant, after saying, "Oh God, not yet, I still have children," it was all gone, and I was back at the ceiling in the hospital room. I did not feel the presence of my angel with me this time. I was looking down at my body on the table. I could see that my eyes were closed, and I watched as they covered part of my body with a blanket.

From the ceiling where I was, I saw my eyes suddenly open. I saw myself look down to the end of the table, then up the left side of my body, above my head, and down my right side. I saw myself, my earthly body scanning the people around the table.

Then just as suddenly, I was in my body lying on the table. I opened my swollen eyes quickly as the nurse at the end of the table exclaimed very loudly, "Mrs. Carter!" I looked down at the end of the table where she was. After all these years, I believe that when she loudly called my name, she also called me back to life, from Eternity in Heaven.

After looking at the end of the table where the nurse was, I then looked along my left side to the top above my head, where a nurse was patting my shoulders. I was doing what I had just seen myself do from the room's ceiling. I saw them all. I was back in my earthly body.

I do not remember much after that. I was either going in and out of consciousness or sleeping from the epinephrine drug they had put in my IV to counter the anaphylaxis. They also transferred me to another room. My family doctor, who had ordered the test to be taken, had been called, and I soon heard his familiar voice. My family doctor exclaimed rather firmly that it was evident that I had an allergic reaction to something. The doctor who had administered the barium said to him, that no one had ever reacted to barium before.

A nurse had called my husband, and the only information she gave him was that his wife needed him. She did not tell him anything else but said that she would meet him at the emergency room door of the hospital. My husband later described what he saw when he entered the room, as a football huddle, and me being the football. He said he was too stunned at what he saw to be scared by what was happening.

At some point, I became aware that my husband was sitting in a chair beside me. He was looking at me as I drifted in and out. I could hear him talking and praying. A nurse was also seated in a chair by my head, and I could hear her talking. She was writing down the vital signs and information. Even though I was going in and out of consciousness and sleeping from the medicine, I could hear what was being said, and I was aware of what was going on around me.

The pain in my stomach had *not* subsided, it was still like labor contractions. The pain and cramps would go from mild to severe and then stop. I would sleep, then they would start again. I would open my eyes off and on as I felt someone touch me or heard different voices of people stopping by for a view. The word had traveled through the lower level of the hospital about the situation. The staff at the hospital wanted to view this woman that had gone into anaphylactic shock and marveled that no one could figure out what had happened to her. I was swollen from head to toe with only slits for my eyes. Not much of my nose was peeking through my face, and I was covered with hives.

It took a couple more hours before the pain in my stomach subsided. I became more awake after three hours had passed, and the medication was wearing off. It was after noon, and I became aware it was getting close to the time for my husband to go to work. My husband was an engineer and drove the train for the Santa Fe Railroad. When he went to work, he would be out of town for two days, and I felt I needed to get home and settled before he left town. I asked the doctor if I could go home, and he said he thought I was through the worse of it. I was allowed to leave the hospital at about two o'clock that Friday afternoon. I remember on the drive home, the sun was so bright my eyes hurt even with them closed. We left my car at the hospital, and my husband took me home to get settled. I was groggy from the medication, weak, and tired, and I went straight to bed. A friend took my husband back to the hospital to get my car before he went to work and would be gone for the next two days.

The Days Following Anaphylaxis

The following morning, twenty-four hours after I went into anaphylactic shock, I was obligated to be at an event a few miles from home. This was on Saturday, February 7, 1987. I walked into the event building, and the first person I saw was the doctor that had administered the barium x-ray to me. He was as shocked to see me as I was to see him. He said that in his thirteen years of practice, he had never had anyone react to the barium, and he hoped that he would never have a day like that again.

After the event, I went home and back to bed and slept. At 4:30 that same Saturday afternoon, I went to the Christian bookstore to pick up a gift before the store closed for the weekend. When I walked into the bookstore, two of the nurses who had attended to me the day before were in the store. One of the nurses exclaimed, "Mrs. Carter! Is that you? You look so much better today. I had prayed for you." The other nurse said, "Our blood pressure was higher than your blood pressure, and we thought we had lost you. Then the nurse called your name, and you opened your eyes. You scared us!"

That same Saturday evening, as I was getting ready to go back to bed, I looked at the clock, and it was 11:20 p.m. The Holy Spirit said to me that I was to tell my experience in Eternity to my Sunday morning class the next morning. I laughed and thought, "But this is a Good Housekeeping story, not a Sunday morning story. You know, when you go in for a medical procedure *well*, and you come out *sick*." The Lord spoke slowly and softly to me, "Don't you remember your angel?" This was the most audible voice I had ever heard, "Remember your angel." My angel? My angel? Yes, my angel! The Holy Spirit started revealing little pieces to me. "Oh God, Oh God!" was all I could say as I sat down on the floor beside my bed and cried. The Holy Spirit then took me step by step back through what I had experienced, seeing my beautiful angel, looking down at my body on the table, seeing my hands and feet, and standing next to His beautiful Shekinah Glory, knowing it was God. The massiveness of the New Jerusalem and the brilliant colors of crystal glass in the walls, seeing the doors, and the strength and design of the cornerstones. The enormous mountain that was inside the walls. The Eternity that is waiting and prepared for us. "Oh, my God," was all I could think and say.

The anaphylaxis had happened on Friday morning, and it was now Saturday night, and the Holy Spirit revealed over and over to me the experience I had in Eternity. Oh, it was so humbling, so beautiful, but exciting.

I spent what seemed like *twenty minutes* in Eternity, but the time on earth had to have been only a couple of minutes. From the time my arms and legs relaxed, someone checking the vital signs, and they thought I had died to the nurse loudly calling out my name, could not have been very long.

The following morning as we were getting ready for church, my husband called from the Santa Fe Railroad yard office. He said he was in town, had gotten off the train, and would do his paperwork. He said he would go home to get ready, and then he would meet us at church.

The Holy Spirit told me again to tell this story to the Sunday morning class. I told the Holy Spirit that He would have to confirm this again to me. I needed to know that I was to tell this incredible, unbelievable story that no one could possibly believe or understand, even though my face and eyes were still swollen from the anaphylaxis.

On the way to church, I asked my children to look in the Book of Revelation and find where something was written about the walls and colors and the three glory gates. I had only been a born-again, spirit-filled Christian for two years, and to refer to and know this was in the Book of Revelation was remarkable in itself. They read to me Revelation 21:12-22. I could not believe it! The scriptures described what I had seen in Eternity. This was just so incredible.

They read Revelation 21:12-14. "It had a great and high wall, with twelve gates, and at each gate were twelve angels, and names were written on them, which are those of the twelve tribes of the sons of Israel. There were three gates on the east and three gates on the north and three gates on the south, and three gates on the west. And the wall of the city had twelve foundation stones, and on them were the twelve names of the twelve apostles of the Lamb."

Revelation 21:16-21, "And the city is laid out as a square, and its length is as great as the width; and he measured the city with a rod, fifteen hundred miles; its length, and width, and height is equal. And he measured its wall, seventy-two yards according to human measurements, which are also angelic measurements. And the material of the wall was jasper, and the city was pure gold, like transparent glass. The foundation stones of the city wall were adorned with every kind of precious stone. And the twelve gates were twelve pearls; each one of the gates was a single pearl." It was hard to get a grasp on what I was hearing. They were reading to me what I had seen.

Our Sunday morning class was in a large room with about seventy-five people. I walked into the room and looked around as the people were starting to gather, and I only knew a few of them. I was thinking to myself, "And I am to tell them what I experienced?" This was way too overwhelming for me. I was so nervous, and my heart was pounding. I found two chairs at a table for my husband and myself. I picked the chair that positioned me behind a man, so I could not see the teacher.

As the teacher started the class, I was still situated behind this man, and I could not see the teacher. When my husband arrived at the classroom door, I was on the other side of the room. I raised my hand halfway up so he would see where I was seated. He went around the room, came up beside me, and sat down. The teacher and others talked, and prayer was said. I thought, "Oh, thank you, Lord, nothing has been confirmed for me to tell this story," and I began to relax.

Suddenly, the teacher leaned to the side of the man blocking my view of her. She pointed her index finger straight at me. Her finger looked like it was a foot long, and she asked if I had something to say. I was so shocked that I looked to see if she was talking to someone sitting behind me. I looked back at her, and she was looking at me. I put my hands up to my chest and said with amazement, "Me?" She asked, "Didn't you have your hand up?" referring to when I motioned to my husband where I was seated. I explained that the Lord had been dealing with me to share something. She asked me to share with the class what the Lord was saying to me. Obediently, I stood up, moved behind my chair to steady myself, and shared with the class the events of the last three days. I do not remember what I said, the Holy Spirit was leading me to speak about the experience.

I thought of my husband seated beside me, hearing this incredible story of going to Eternity for the first time.

After class, my husband and I went to the church sanctuary, and our children went from their classes to the children's church. I did not stop to talk to anyone. I went straight to where we usually sat while my husband stopped to speak with several people. The nurse that had been with us at the hospital, who was sitting by us and writing down all the information, came running up to my husband. He was very shocked to see her. My husband came into the church sanctuary and sat down beside me. He was as white as a sheet, quiet, and very stunned at what he had heard in class and also by seeing the nurse.

Later that afternoon, he told me that he could not believe the nurse sitting beside us that morning in the hospital was in our church. They both had been praying for me, and the power of prayer is evident when two or more are praying together. The scripture in Matthew 18:19 states, "Again, I say to you, that if two of you agree on earth about anything that they may ask, it shall be done for them by My Father who is in Heaven." They had been praying for me individually and together, even though they did not know it. For the next few days, my husband and I were both numb and overwhelmed about what had happened over the past few days. God put four people that had attended to me in the hospital on Friday morning back in my path the following two days, Saturday and Sunday.

I believe God was confirming that everything I went through with the anaphylaxis and everything I saw in Eternity had happened. Seeing these four people the following days was not a coincidence. God knew I would need the reassurance. He also knew the evil one would try to kill, steal, or destroy what God had shown me. God knew I would need evidence and reassurance for myself, that it did indeed happen, and that what happened was from Him.

On Tuesday, four days after the anaphylaxis at the hospital, I went to the women's Bible study group in the chapel of our church that I regularly attended. My Sunday morning teacher and another lady came running up to me. They wanted me to tell my story in the Bible study class that morning. I said sure, then prayer started, and we sat down.

During prayer, the devil gave me all the reasons I was not worthy for this to have happened to me. Why would He choose you? Who do you think you are? You are not anyone special!

After prayer, I told the two ladies I could not tell this story. They ushered me into a small room off the chapel. I told them what the evil one had said to me. After that day, I asked God, on several occasions, that same series of questions. Why would He choose me? I was nobody and indeed not anyone special. His answer to me was plain and simple, "Because you are my child."

In that room off the chapel, both ladies laid hands on me, anointed me with oil, and prayed over me. They prayed for me and about God taking me to see Eternity. My teacher prayed that this story would be shared only when it was supposed to be shared and only with whom it was supposed to be shared. This prayer was very evident as the years passed.

In that room, God said to me, "My people are not ready yet." God told me to seal this story up and put it on the shelf until the time was right when His people would understand. In my spirit, I put my unbelievable story in a clear glass jar, put the lid on it, sealed it, and set the jar on the shelf in that room by the chapel. I sealed up my story just like God had told Daniel to do. And there, in that room by the chapel, His story stayed. I had no idea it would be twenty-five years before God would release His story to be revealed and shared openly.

When I wanted to be alone or in prayer with God, my mind and thoughts would go to that beautiful place in Eternity to see, feel, breathe, and be in God's glory. It enriched my prayer life to a new level.

Praise and worship became so much more powerful and beautiful. I was amazed by the number of songs that were about our eternal home. It was a new awakening for me to hear and understand the praise and worship songs in a new light and dimension. There is such a difference between when we are just singing a song and when we are really praising and worshipping our Lord Jesus, the Messiah, Yeshua, and Yahweh.

This was a difficult experience for my flesh to talk about. You would think I would have wanted to shout it from the rooftops and tell everyone what I saw, but that was not how it was. God told me to seal it up until the time was right. God had entrusted me with this incredible experience, and I felt I could not and should not share it with just anyone. I kept it very close to my heart and protected it. I had a responsibility to God for what He had given me.

Matthew 7:6 tells us, "Do not give what is holy to dogs and do not throw your pearls before swine, lest they trample them under their feet, and turn and tear you to pieces." Dogs refer to the ungodly, wicked men or fools. Swine refers to deceived people or backsliders. We can witness to everyone about Jesus, but we should be careful with sacred things about God or from God that He has given us. We cannot give something as precious as a pearl to someone who would not appreciate it, and *this was my pearl.*

In 2 Corinthians 12:1-5, Apostle Paul is speaking to the Corinthians. He said it is not profitable to boast about himself, but it is necessary in order to answer the Corinthians' questions. Paul said he would continue boasting about his visions and revelations. "Boasting is necessary though it is not profitable, but I, Paul will go on to speak of visions and revelations of the Lord" (2 Corinthians 12:1).

Paul would talk about himself, but again it was easier for Paul to speak as if it were about someone else. Paul says, "I know a man in Christ who fourteen years ago, whether in the body I do not know, or out of the body I do not know, God knows such a man, was caught up to the third heaven" (2 Corinthians 12:2). The third heaven is where God dwells.

Paul is saying he knows such a man. Of course, Paul is talking about himself. It is difficult, says Paul, to talk about what happened to him going to the third Heaven. Paul states, "And I know how such a man, whether in the body or apart from the body I do not know, God knows, was caught up into Paradise/Heaven and heard inexpressible words, which a man is not permitted to speak" (2 Corinthians 12:3-4). Not being permitted to speak means that an earthly human could not express the true meaning of what he saw in Heaven.

Paul then states he would boast about the vision if it were someone else's vision. But about himself, it is hard for him to speak. Paul can only speak about his own weaknesses. Paul says, "On behalf of such a man will I boast; but on my own behalf, I will not boast, except in regard to my weaknesses" (2 Corinthians 12:5). Paul says it would be foolish for him to boast, but if he does speak, he will be speaking the truth. Paul will not speak of it easily because he does not want to be credited with more than he is. In 2 Corinthians 12:6, Paul says, "For if I do wish to boast, I shall not be foolish, for I shall be speaking the truth; but I refrain from this, so that no one may credit me with more than he sees in me or hears from me." Paul was humble and had a low view of his own importance.

I understand Paul and these scriptures so well. It is very difficult for me to speak about my experience of going to Eternity. I could easily talk about it if it had happened to someone else. We all know it is easier to ask for prayer for someone else than to ask for prayer for ourselves.

I talked about my experience and going to Eternity only when prompted by the Holy Spirit. It happened two, maybe three times a year for the next twenty-five years. Sometimes, the experience God gave me would just come out when I was talking to someone. I always knew it was for a reason. God wanted to reach them, talk to them, heal them, or give them comfort about a loved one. I never really knew why I would tell the story when I did, but I always knew God had a reason, or I would not have spoken about it.

Each time I spoke about it, people's reactions were the same. They did not have many facial expressions and did not say much after I finished telling of the experience. I knew they had to process what the Holy Spirit had just revealed to them. They had just experienced something profound, and there was nothing much for either of us to say. I had also just revealed a very personal part of myself. I always trusted and believed God had His reasons.

One fact about this gift God has given to me of going to Eternity is that I do not care what people think of me or about me. I know what I have seen and experienced.

Life after My Death

This experience changed my life and the lives of my husband and children. My husband and I lived for the next five years after the anaphylaxis incident, not knowing what had happened to cause the anaphylaxis or if it would happen again. How much time would God give me on earth? We have always been told to live as if Jesus is coming today but plan for tomorrow. This took on a new meaning for me.

I dug deep into the Word to know more about who Jesus is. We started doing special activities, spending more quality time together, and taking family vacations. We started making memories that we might have put off until later or until our children were older. I did not know how long I would have with my children. What I thought at the time was that God had granted my request to return to raise our children.

My husband and I started living life a little differently than we would have had I not had this experience. Things we would not have even thought about doing together until after our retirement, we started doing. Retiring together did not seem like an option anymore. Putting things off for another day, another time did not seem like an option, either. Time was precious and short, and I wanted to get the most out of every day. Again, living as if Jesus is coming today but planning for tomorrow. Life and time was extremely important, and I did not want to miss anything or leave a stone unturned. I always said, "let no moss grow under my feet."

The Holy Spirit began giving me an unquenchable desire to travel and see the world. Travel was something He put on my heart and soul. I knew I had to do it but did not know why. When my husband and I first started our travels, my husband told me it was challenging for him to leave home, and I knew it was. I told him I understood his uneasiness about traveling, but he had to realize that I had to go. Travel was like a burning desire within me.

The beauty our God has created on this earth is indescribable and never ceases to amaze me. Now, as I look back, it was like He wanted me to see all His creation, all His magnificent beauty. I believe He especially wanted me to meet people from all over the world. What I learned was that everyone is basically the same. The culture, the country, and the language might be different, but we were all created the same by Him. Our travels also helped me to understand the countries I would later study.

The Good Housekeeping Magazine

I had gone through several different kinds of allergy tests after the anaphylaxis. The doctor always thought there was something in the barium liquid that I was allergic to. He had the barium analyzed to see what might have been in it that would have caused my reaction. We had no success in understanding or an explanation for why it had happened.

It was *five years* after my experience that we finally found out why I had gone into anaphylactic shock. Five long years! I did not think we were ever going to know the cause of the anaphylaxis. In the March 1992 issue of The Good Housekeeping magazine, there was an article, "The Case of the Mystery Epidemic." The article told the stories of people who had gone into anaphylactic shock and described their symptoms. This was the first time I had read or heard any explanation or description of anaphylaxis. This was a revelation for me to read. *Finally*, there might be an explanation and answer to why I experienced anaphylaxis.

There were several stories over a span of three years that were talked about in the article. Several women had gone into anaphylactic shock when having a barium x-ray. They were saying the tip of the barium tube was latex, and this was the cause of the anaphylaxis.

One such story was this: A technician inserted a catheter in a patient's rectum and left to find the radiologist. She began sweating profusely, her heart was beating wildly, and her throat began constricting. She called out to the technician, then slipped in and out of consciousness. The technician came back with the doctor. Barely conscious, she heard them discussing her. "She seemed fine when she came in, but she did ask if anyone had ever reacted to barium. We have not even started the barium flow," the technician said. The doctor removed the catheter, and she felt him slip a blood pressure cuff on her arm. "My God, her systolic is only eighty! Let's get her into ICU." She lost consciousness as she was carried to the ICU.

According to the articles, during this same time period, an allergist at the Children's Hospital of Wisconsin found ten patients who had gone into anaphylaxis in six months. He started searching indexes of medical journals dating back five years and found several patients who suffered allergic reactions before surgery. Some of the patient's reports concluded they were allergic to latex.

This made sense. Latex rubber was everywhere in the operating room. Latex rubber was used to make the mask that delivers the anesthetic, and all the gloves were latex at that time. Latex particles slough off into the air when a box of gloves is opened. The article went on to say the Food and Drug Administration had received reports that sixty women had died from anaphylaxis during barium enemas, many of whom began to react before the barium flow was started.

The Good Housekeeping articles described what had happened to these women. The tip was latex which caused the anaphylactic shock that caused the death of these *sixty* women. These stories were overwhelming, but it was such a relief to understand the cause of the anaphylaxis. Latex allergy is now a new killer, the article stated! The mystery was solved, the epidemic was latex allergy. Latex is a lot like penicillin, it is valuable, but for a few people, it can be deadly.

What happened to me when I was thirty-eight years old was an allergic reaction to latex. The tip of the barium tube was latex. I went into anaphylactic shock, died on the table, went to Eternity, and God gave me the time to come back. Not everyone was as fortunate as I was. So many died before they discovered that latex was the cause of the deaths. If I had officially been declared dead that day, I would *not have* even been a statistic. It was over three years after my incident that researchers started putting together that there was a latex reaction from the tip of the tube used when giving a barium x-ray. Learning what had caused my anaphylactic shock gave us relief. We now knew latex had caused my reaction and could possibly prevent something like this from happening again.

After I found this information about the latex tip, I contacted the doctor's office that had given me the barium x-ray. I wanted to share this information with them. The doctor's office said they had no record of such an incident happening. I figured they were afraid of a lawsuit or something, so they denied it ever happening. I did not pursue the issue. I assumed that after five years, they were most likely aware of the situation with latex.

One time when I was waiting in the allergist's office, I saw a book on latex allergy on the doctor's shelf. I took the book down to glance through it and found that by 1995, eight years after my anaphylaxis, there had been one hundred and fifty deaths attributed to the barium latex tip. Oh wow, that was just unbelievable that so many had experienced this and did not live through it. This was heartbreaking for me, and also to think of how many others like myself had experienced this situation, lived through it, and did not know why or what had caused them to go into anaphylaxis. It was a relief for me to now understand what had happened and why. This information also gave me symptoms to recognize. I had to get used to the idea of looking for anything that might contain latex and taking precautions. At that time, every doctor and dentist's office still used latex examination gloves. I was in the dentist's office, and I forgot to say something before they put on their regular latex gloves. I immediately started the allergic reaction with my lips and face tingling, then my eyes itching, and my throat started constricting. After that, my allergy to latex was written in big, bold red letters on my dentist chart. It was something I had to start watching for, it was not a one-time allergy to latex incident. It would happen again, as I learned throughout life.

In those early years, before latex was widely known, one of my family's concerns was if I was in a severe car accident and the paramedics would use latex gloves on an open area. My family and the doctor wanted me to wear a bracelet to identify the latex allergy. I did wear a bracelet for a short time, but I carried an epinephrine injection pen for years.

I was in and out of the allergist's office several times after the anaphylaxis. The severity of the allergy reaction to latex had compromised my immune system. I had allergy issues that I did not have before the anaphylaxis, which mostly consisted of skin allergies and irritations to the skin. As the doctor told me, my skin is an organ, and my immune system for my skin had been compromised. I have taken a daily allergy prescription for years, and it keeps it under control.

One perspective I received from this incident is that I am not afraid of dying. It is the unknown of how we are going to die that makes us frightened of death. It is also the feeling of loss, of not being there as our children grow and leaving behind the people we love.

My husband, my youngest daughter, and I talked very openly about my experience and what would happen if God called me back. I thought for many years that He had let me return to finish raising my children. I did not realize it then, but now I believe God would not take me back until His plan was finished with His story.

Looking back, I know I lived on the edge of the what-ifs in life. What if I am called back? What if I am not here to see my grandchildren? What if my husband and I did not get to live out our life together? Every experience in our lives impacts us in some way, and this is how I was impacted.

What was in my future? Why would I experience such a life-changing event and be told to *seal it up* if God was not going to do something with it? I later studied the Book of Daniel, where God told Daniel to *seal it up* and for Daniel to *go on his way*. The scripture is in Daniel 12:4, "But for you, Daniel, conceal these words and *seal up* the book *until the end of time*; many will go back and forth, and knowledge will increase."

This scripture really spoke to me. I was to go on with my life, and I was to follow the Holy Spirit's directions. God would take care of everything in His own timing. I did not even see the words until the end of time in the scripture until I was studying the Book of Daniel again to teach it.

I continued with life. I worked, raised my family, and was blessed with grandchildren. I did have to retire from work earlier than I wanted or expected because of my skin allergies. After retiring, I took up the hobby of genealogy. Genealogy taught me how to use the computer efficiently and how to search and research for information and to get the truth. Even during this time, there was a plan in place that I did not know about.

I have never read any books on the topic of people going to Heaven. I have not watched or listened to anyone give their testimony about going to Heaven. The Holy Spirit told me to keep my experience pure as to where I went and what I saw.

You probably cannot go through life without hearing about someone who has gone to Heaven. I have heard stories that some people have seen Jesus, seen their loved ones, and seen their unborn or aborted babies in Heaven. I have heard people have seen their known and unknown ancestors in Heaven. People ask me, did I see this, or did I see that while I was in Heaven? Heaven is a big place, and I believe people have been to different parts and seen different things in Heaven. Some say they have experienced music, smelling beautiful smells, or seeing beautiful flowers. I want you to know that I believe their stories are true. But I always wonder if an angel was involved, because I believe, after having my experience, that an angel does escort us to Heaven. I also believe that I went to a different place in Heaven. I went to Eternity, and not the present Heaven most people say they went to. You will learn in our study that there is a difference between Heaven and Eternity.

Other Experiences

I have been asked if I have ever had any other experiences. The answer is that I have had other situations where I believe my angel was watching over me, and God intervened.

When I was twenty-one years old, I had a car accident. I rolled my car three times and landed on the other side of the highway. The car was upside down with the top crushed in. I saw "the white, bright tunnel" with the bright light at the end. I never knew how I got out of the car. I walked away with only a few scratches from that incident.

I had back surgery, and the surgery was a success for the back pain, but something happened during the surgery. When I woke up, I had no feeling in my left leg, ankle, or foot. I had no movement or function of my left leg. I left the hospital using a walker, not knowing if I would ever walk again. I fell three months after surgery, injured the same left ankle, and broke my left wrist. I had surgery on my wrist, and a plate was put in. My wrist, ankle, and foot were both put in a brace. I used a cane for quite a while and have experienced several falls because of my weak left leg. With God's healing, physical therapy, and time, I have fully recovered.

Another time I had a stomachache for several hours before I boarded an airplane for a six-hour flight. When we landed in Los Angeles, California, I was very sick. An ambulance was called to the airport, and I was transferred to the local hospital. There I underwent emergency surgery. My intestine had twisted and clamped off like a napkin in a napkin ring. The surgeon told us before surgery that because the intestine had been clamped off for too many hours, part of the intestine had likely died from the lack of blood supply and would probably have to be removed. The doctor told me that *if* I made it through the surgery, I would probably lose that part of my intestine, and I would probably have to wear a colostomy bag for the rest of my life.

My husband immediately called several friends for prayer, and my situation went out on our prayer chain. The doctor did not remove any intestine, and I did not have a colostomy bag. This incident happened while I was teaching a four-month session on the Book of Revelation.

All doctors and staff were informed and cautioned about the latex allergy in my back, wrist, and stomach surgery. The surgery rooms were carefully prepared, searched, and researched for any latex products, and a crash cart was always there. When I was in the hospital for these surgeries, signs stating NO latex were put above my bed, on the door, and on my charts. Each time I was in the hospital, a nurse would ask me what warranted all the latex signs. They would completely understand after I told them about the anaphylactic shock situation.

These were all serious incidents that happened to me where my life was spared. Nothing compares to my experience in Eternity, but these were supernatural interventions in my life, that I believe, were directed by God as well. What the enemy meant for harm God used for good.

Chapter Two

✧✧✧

STUDYING THE BOOK OF REVELATION

IN 2014, THE Holy Spirit put a desire in my heart to learn more about the end times and the Book of Revelation. Our pastor, Jimmy Evans, had talked about the end of times for quite a while, and it piqued my interest. I wanted to know more about what the Bible said would take place in the future. What were the end-time events, and what would take place during the Tribulation?

This started me on an adventurous, exciting study of the Book of Revelation. At first, I found the Book of Revelation very difficult to understand. I began by familiarizing myself with end-time words like "revelation," meaning to take the cover off and reveal the "glory" of Jesus Christ. "Glory" the beauty of His spirit. "Apocalypse" the Greek word for revelation, meaning to uncover or unveil knowledge. "Eschatology" the study of the end times. These were exciting words, and they were telling me something was to be revealed and uncovered in the Book of Revelation, and I wanted to find out what it was.

The Holy Spirit instructed me on how I was to study the Book of Revelation. I was to take each scripture and type it on the computer. Then take the scripture apart, and unpack it word by word until I understood what each word meant and what the scripture was telling me. I was to do this with every word and every scripture in the Book of Revelation.

I began by comparing the same scripture in several different versions of the Bible and all the footnotes in each version. I used the Hebrew- Greek Key Word New American Standard Bible, which explained what some of the words meant in Greek. The Greek meaning gave an even deeper understanding of the words or at least a synonym of the word. Some Bibles put other scripture references next to the scripture for similar themes or meanings. I also used this process of letting other scriptures help to explain the meaning of scripture.

The Book of Revelation uses many He, Him, they, and them, which confused me regarding who was being talked about. I would write the scripture using He/Jesus or they/the angels. This helped me to keep everyone straight in the scripture. I found this much fun and enjoyed my time each day researching the scriptures. I enjoyed what the Book of Revelation was telling me. I also read other books and watched videos on the end times. I wanted to learn what the scholars had to say about the prophecies in the Book of Revelation and what they had to say about the end times. I gathered all the information I could in my study.

It took me over ten months to break down and unpack all the scriptures in the Book of Revelation. Separating, breaking down, and unpacking a scripture word by word was necessary for me to understand what the scripture was telling me. I looked up each word in the scripture and wrote the word on the computer, followed by the meaning. I separated the verse between the commas into smaller portions to research it. This is how I broke down scripture to understand it.

Breaking Down the Scripture Word by Word

I use the New American Standard Bible, but I always check other versions, including the King James Version. Let us start with the first scripture in the Book of Revelation and see what it tells us.

Revelation 1:1 (NAS), "The Revelation of Jesus Christ, which God gave Him to show to His bond-servants, the things which must shortly take place; and He sent and communicated it by His angel to His bond-servant John."

This scripture is packed full of information that needs a further explanation for a better understanding. Taking the first part of this scripture from the beginning to the first comma, I started breaking the scripture down.

The Revelation of Jesus Christ, let us find out what this means word by word.

1. *Revelation:* to take the cover off of something hidden and to reveal it. The Greek word for revelation is the *apocalypse,* meaning uncovering and unveiling. So, the word revelation is to uncover and reveal something hidden.

2. *Of:* means about or from.

3. *Jesus Christ:* means Savior of the world. Jesus, the one called Christ, is the son of God, the Messiah. Jesus inaugurates and controls the experience of salvation. Christ is the revelation or revealing of God. If you have seen me/Jesus, you have seen the Father/God (John 14:9).

We can now understand this portion and the meaning of **The Revelation of Jesus Christ**. It is the revealing, the uncovering *about* Jesus Christ. God is going to reveal Jesus to us. This should get you as excited as it did me. The first five words tell us that God reveals Jesus to us in the Book of Revelation.

The second set of words between the commas are: **which God gave Him to show to His bond-servants**. This is what I was talking about earlier when I said the Bible uses so many He and Him references. I needed to know exactly who was being referred to, to keep them straight.

1. *which God:* God means the supreme Divinity, the Lord God.

2. *gave Him:* Him is referring to Jesus here.

3. *to show:* means communicating to, or revealing to someone. God gave to Jesus.

4. *His;* is referring to God here.

5. *bond-servants:* there is more than one bond-servant because it is plural. Bond-servants implies obedience, devotion, and spoken of the faithful followers and worshippers. A servant of God is either

an agent sent from God as Moses was sent or the worshipper of God, us, the believers.

Now understanding this part of the verse is more apparent, **which God gave Him to show to His bond-servants**. Which God, gave to Him/Jesus to show and to reveal to His/God's followers. So, God revealed something to Jesus, and Jesus is revealing something to us, the believers.

The third set of words between the commas are: **the things which must shortly take place**,

1. *the things:* mean the secrets or mysteries. Daniel 2:28 tells us that there is a God in Heaven who reveals mysteries and secrets that will take place in the latter days.
2. *which must:* means something has to happen and will happen.
3. *shortly:* means speedily, quickly, or suddenly. This does not mean it has to happen soon, but when things do begin to happen, they will happen swiftly and quickly. Revelation 3:11 states, "I am coming quickly," this is not necessarily soon, but when Jesus does come, it will be swift and speedily.
4. *take place:* which means it must happen.

Now we see a more precise meaning of, **the things which must shortly take place**. The secrets and mysteries, which must happen, very rapidly, will happen. God is saying that when God reveals the secrets and mysteries about Himself, it will be done very quickly.

The last set of words between the comma to the end are: **and He sent and communicated it by His angel to His bond-servant John.**

1. *and He sent:* here He is stating that Jesus sent something.
2. *and communicated:* means to make something known.
3. *It:* means the message, the secrets.
4. *by His angel:* His refers to Jesus's angel. Jesus has His own angel.
5. *to;* means to show and reveal the secret.
6. *His:* His here refers to Jesus.
7. *bond-servant John:* John is God's follower and messenger.

In this part of the scripture, **and He sent and communicated it by His angel to His bond-servant John**. Jesus sent and communicated, made known, to Jesus's angel the message, and Jesus's angel is going to show and reveal the message to God's bond-servant, John. Jesus will give this message to His very own angel, and His angel will tell this message to Apostle John.

We will reread the scripture of Revelation 1:1, with the <u>explanation following each word</u>.

The Revelation (uncovering and revealing) of (or about) Jesus Christ (our Savior), which God (the Deity) gave Him (Jesus) to show (and tell) to His (God) bond-servants (the followers), the things (the secrets and mysteries) which must (or has to) shortly (quickly) take place (meaning has to happen); and He (Jesus) sent and communicated it (made known the message) by His (Jesus's own) angel to His (God) bond-servant (faithful follower) John.

This gives a clearer understanding of the scripture. God will reveal the message to Jesus, Jesus reveals the message to His own angel, the angel reveals it to John, and John will deliver that message, the secret, to us through the Book of Revelation. Apostle John is the revealer of the Book of Revelation to us.

For ten months, I researched, deciphered, broke down, took apart, and unpacked the words and scriptures of the Book of Revelation, as I revealed above. I took events like the Tribulation, the Seven-Sealed Scroll, the Seven Judgments, and the Abomination of Desolation. I wrote an abundance of information on each one of these events. I was understanding what John was revealing and uncovering. The knowledge of secrets is to be revealed in the end times, and we are in the end times now.

The Book of Revelation is the *only* book in the Bible with a *promise* that is given, if you read, hear, and heed (pay attention or take notice) of the Word. Revelation 1:3, "Blessed is he who reads and those who hear the words of the prophecy, and heed the things which are written in it; for the time is near." We are promised we will be blessed by reading and hearing the Book of Revelation with the condition that we take notice of the words of the prophecy.

Teaching the Book of Revelation

After this intense study, the Lord called me to teach the Book of Revelation to others so they could understand it. I asked our pastor for permission to use a room in the church to have a women's study group on the Book of Revelation.

I taught the Book of Revelation twice a year for the next five years and a couple of sessions in our Sunday morning class. I also taught a course on the Book of Daniel. Daniel is significant in understanding the Book of Revelation. The Book of Daniel is to the Old Testament what the Book of Revelation is to the New Testament in terms of prophecy. I have repeatedly been asked to teach again, but teaching was for that season. Seven years have passed since teaching, and now the Holy Spirit has called me to write this book.

How This Book Was Birthed

I was asked to give my testimony to our home group of about fifty people. Many in this group had known me for years but did not know I had gone to Eternity. After much response and interest from the group, I felt the Holy Spirit wanted me to do a deeper study and learn more about our future in the Afterlife. What happens when we die, where do we go, and what will we see in the Afterlife? When I came back from Eternity, I already had an understanding of the Afterlife that I cannot explain.

The Holy Spirit started stirring in me, things were changing within me again, excitement was building after giving my testimony. A small quiet voice said it was time to write a book. This was the first time I had been told to write a book. It had been thirty-five years since I went to Eternity. The message was sealed for twenty-five years until the Lord had me study and teach the Book of Revelation. Then another seven years before He said to write this book.

The Trip

Do you want to know what happens and what will take place after we die? Some do, and some say Jesus will take care of it. Well, for us curious ones, we need to know more about what happens after our life on this earth is completed.

We plan and prepare before we take any trip, and we are going to go on the most extensive and exciting trip of our life. There is the who, what, when, and where of every trip we take. This is the same way I feel about our Afterlife. We need to plan, prepare, and know what will happen in our Afterlife. How can we witness to others if we, the Christian believers, do not know what is going to take place after our life on this earth is completed?

1. Where are we going? We are first going to Heaven, then the Millennial Kingdom, and then to Eternity.

2. Who is going? All the believers in Jesus Christ.

3. What are we taking? We will take absolutely nothing with us.

4. When are we going? We will die on this earth and go to Heaven, or we will go in the Rapture.

5. How are we going? We will go in our new resurrected and glorified bodies made for eternal life.

6. How do we prepare? We store up our treasures in Heaven.

7. How long are we going to be there? We will be in Heaven for at least seven years. We will be in the Millennium for one thousand years and in Eternity forever.

8. What are we going to do when we get there? In Heaven, we will receive our rewards and crowns. We will praise and worship Jesus and have a beautiful banquet. Then we will rule and reign with Jesus in the Millennium for one thousand years. In Eternity we will be with Jesus and God forever in a new city and on a new Earth.

A lot of what I mentioned above, some may not fully understand, but you will learn and understand as we study every one of these events.

The Afterlife

The first question you must ask yourself is, "Do I have salvation through Jesus Christ?" The answer to this question determines everything for your Afterlife and eternal existence. The dictionary defines the word Afterlife as existence after death, a later period of one's life. The Afterlife is the unending existence after death. Synonyms for the word Afterlife are beyond, the hereafter, and immortality. The definition of eternal is infinite time, duration without end, and lasting or existing forever.

Our Afterlife takes place when our life on this present earth is complete. Psalm 90:10 states, "As for the days of our life, they contain seventy years, or if due to strength, eighty years." Our life on this earth is such a short time compared to the eternal life waiting for us.

For the believer in Jesus, we will be absent from the body and present with the Lord at the moment of death. Philippians 3:20, "For our *citizenship* is in heaven, where we eagerly wait for a Savior, the Lord Jesus Christ." This is encouraging to know our citizenship is in Heaven with Jesus and not on this earth.

When a person dies, that person will go to one of two places, Heaven or Hell. There is no third option or place. We are eternal beings, and there is no such thing as soul annihilation or complete destruction. When we die on this earth, the decision is final. We will have everlasting life in Heaven or live forever in Hell.

Chapter Three

◇◇◇◇

THE THREE HEAVENS

LET US START with the three heavens that are above the earth. Deuteronomy 10:14 refers to *three heavens* in one verse: "Behold, to the Lord your God, belongs heaven (2nd heaven), and the highest heavens of Heavens (3rd heaven), and the earth and all that is in it (1st heaven)."

During our time on earth, we dwell in the first two heavens. The first Heaven above earth is the atmospheric heaven. This contains the things we see, birds, clouds, and where the airplanes fly.

The second Heaven is far away, but we can see some of it. This second Heaven is known as the celestial or stellar Heaven. This part of Heaven includes the sun, moon, and stars. The second Heaven is where Satan and his demons dwell. It is a place where spiritual warfare takes place. In Daniel 10:12-14, God told Daniel that He (God) answered Daniel's prayers in the third heaven (where God dwells) on the first day Daniel prayed, but it was delayed by conflict in the second heaven for twenty-one days. Satan held up Daniel's prayers in the second Heaven. Satan and his demons dwell between us on earth and God, Who is in the third Heaven. The third Heaven is where God is on His throne. Isaiah 14:13 tells us that Heaven is above the clouds, above the stars of God in the recesses of the *north*. No matter what part of the earth you are on, this scripture says always look to the *north* for Heaven.

Heaven, Used in the Broad Term

When we use the word "Heaven," we are usually referring to that beautiful place we all hear about, where our believing ancestors, parents, family, and friends have gone. As believers, we know we will go to Heaven when we die, or we will go to Heaven in the Rapture. Many use the terms Heaven and Eternity interchangeably without knowing these are two different places and take place at two different times.

The word "Heaven" is a broad term for three different places we will go in our Afterlife. The present Heaven, the Millennium, and Eternity. Using the word "Heaven" for one or all three of these places is not wrong or incorrect. However, we will learn and understand that they are three different places that occur at three different times in the Afterlife.

The present Heaven is the first place we will go after death or in the Rapture. The present Heaven is a temporary place, we will not stay in the present Heaven forever. We will remain in the present Heaven until Jesus makes His Second Return at the end of the seven years of Tribulation. After His Second Coming, we will move into the Millennial Kingdom, the second place of our Afterlife. After the one thousand years of the Millennial Kingdom, we will enter Eternity forever.

Heaven is God's Dwelling Place

When Jesus left the earth, He went to prepare a place for the believer. Jesus tells us in John 14:2-3 (KJV), "In My Father's <u>house</u>, there are many <u>mansions</u>: if it were not so, I would have told you so. I will go to prepare a _____. And if I go and prepare a place for you, <u>I will come again</u>, and receive you unto myself; that where I am, there you will be also."

Jesus also makes quite a statement here. Jesus says, where I am going, there you will also be. He is not just saying where you, the believers go, I will be there, but where I/Jesus go, you will go. Jesus is leading, and He is taking us to be with Him.

Let me explain the words in the scripture John 14:2-3 that I underlined:

1. House: the Greek word is *oikia*, meaning dwelling place. The Father's house is His dwelling place in Heaven.

2. Mansion: the Greek word is *mone*, which means an abiding place or an abode, a dwelling place.

3. Place for you: the Greek word is *topos*, which is a place of habitation, as a city.

Mansions are defined as dwelling places, abodes, and resting areas in God's residence. I believe we misunderstand the word mansion and think of something only our human mind can define as a mansion. Our earthly mind thinks of a place with everything our earthly person would ever want, with everything in it, our dream house. Yes, it will be the most beautiful place we have ever seen, but the word mansion here means a dwelling place, an abode, a living place for us in Heaven.

In John 14:2 in the King James Bible, the word mansion refers to Jesus' followers being welcomed into everlasting habitation in His Father's house. This same scripture in the New American Standard and several other versions of the Bible use the Greek word *oikia* meaning dwelling place, instead of the word mansion. A dwelling place is used in the sense of rooms. There will be many rooms or dwelling places in His Father's house.

The use of mansion, in Greek, translates as a house, meaning an abode by implication of a family. The word translates as mansions, rooms, or apartments implying the act of staying or residing. Putting the Greek words together, Jesus is saying that in God's dwelling place in Heaven, there will be many people in the family of God, all abiding together. Within God's heavenly house, Christian believers will live in the presence of the Lord. This is quite different from the idea of rows of earthly mansions, the image many people picture.

John 14:3 (KJV) "And if I go and prepare a place for you, I will come again, and receive you unto Myself; that where I am, there you may be also."

1. I will come again: This refers to the Rapture, not the Second Coming.

2. Receive you unto Myself: Since Christ is in Heaven, that is where we are going at the time of our death or in the Rapture.

3. Where I am, there you will be: Where Jesus is, there we will be. He is going to prepare a place for His people.

There is still more to this scripture. Jesus' disciple, Thomas, said to Him, "Lord, we do not know where You are going, how do we know the way?" Jesus said to Thomas, "I am the way, and the truth, and the life, no one comes to the Father except through Me" (John 14:5-6). Jesus knows the way, and He will come again to get us and take us with Him!

Jesus Died for Our Sins

We cannot be saved until we realize in our own hearts that we are a sinner, separated from the love of God. We have to know that our salvation is through the death of Jesus Christ on the cross, that He was raised again in three days and now sits at the <u>right hand</u> of God the Father (1 Corinthians 15:4; Romans 6:9; Hebrews 12:2).

The right hand is very important, it means the place of honor, status, power, and authority. Sitting at the right hand of God means Jesus has the same authority and equal status to His Father in the Godhead. Later we will see that Jesus takes the Seven-Sealed Scroll out of the powerful right hand of God and takes the authority to open the Scroll. We take an oath and lay our right hand on the Bible in the court of law. In the olden days, people would use a right handshake as a sign of their word, a sign of agreement, or a binding contract. The right-hand means authority and power.

Jesus was born to a virgin named Mary. He was born as a human into this sinful world, but Jesus did not sin. He lived a life of perfect submission to the will of His Father, God. Jesus is the Messiah, the Christ, the Son of God, who was crucified for the sins of humanity before rising from the dead. Jesus is the Godhead, the Father, Son, and Holy Spirit. Jesus, who knew no sin, became sin on our behalf. He was payment for us so that we might have righteousness, meaning the right standing with God. Jesus Christ came to pay the penalty for our sins (2 Corinthians 5:21).

Galatians 1:3-4 states, "The Lord Jesus Christ who gave Himself for our sins that He might deliver us out of this present evil age, according to the will of our God and Father." Jesus gave Himself for our iniquities and sins. He paid the penalty and provided the payment for us.

Christ redeemed us from the curse of the Law (the Old Testament sacrifices). He did that by becoming a payment for us, standing in for our sins. "While we were still helpless, at the right time Christ died for the ungodly" (Romans 5:6-8). This is the unique message of the Gospel, the good news of Jesus Christ. Jesus died for us. He paid for us and our sins.

Christ is our Passover, our passing over death and destruction. Jesus was sacrificed for our sins. We shall never die if our salvation is in Jesus (1 Corinthians 5:7).

Crucifixion on the cross usually caused people to die from suffocation. No act of man or nature took the life of Jesus. Jesus gave up His spirit and His life. He surrendered His life to God for us. Mark 15:37 states, "Jesus uttered a loud cry and breathed His last." Jesus gave up His spirit, His life for us, and to take our sins upon Himself. Matthew 27:50 states, "Jesus cried out again with a loud voice, and yielded up His spirit."

We will learn more about Jesus dying for us, when we study Sheol and Hades.

Jesus was called the King of the Jews and the King of Israel. We have a Jewish Messiah and a Jewish Bible from a church founded by the Jewish leadership. If you are Jewish, be proud of your Jewish heritage.

My Jewish family name is Kohn. My great-great-grandfather Louis Kohn came to America in 1860 from Bohemia, Prussia. The Kohn lineage is from the tribe of Levi.

What Are We Made Of?

It is important to know what we are made of. The human being is made up of the body, the soul, and the spirit. The **soul** is who we are. Our soul consists of our mind, thoughts, character, and feelings. Our soul can be self- centered, and it houses our ego. Our soul interacts with the things around us. This means using our five senses, the sense of sight, hearing, taste, smell, and touch. Souls belong to the Lord. He created our souls when He created us in our mother's womb. The soul will never die.

"The lamp of the body is the eye. If your eye is clear, your whole body will be full of light. But if your eye is bad, your whole body will be full of darkness" (Matthew 6:22-23). The eyes are the windows to our souls.

We cannot be distracted by the things on this earth. We cannot take our possessions on earth with us in the Afterlife. It would be senseless to want to gain the whole world but lose one's soul. Our soul's destination, that is, our mind, thoughts, and character, is of great importance and should be the priority in a person's life.

Our spirit is the part of us that connects, communicates, and nurtures our relationship with God. Only believers are said to be spiritually alive (1 Corinthians 2:11; James 2:26; Hebrews 4:12), while unbelievers are considered spiritually dead (Ephesians 2:1-5; Colossians 2:13).

Without the spirit's work in us, we cannot know the Lord and understand His Word. The spirit belongs to God. John 3:6 states, "That which is born of the flesh is flesh." This is our physical birth, and "That which is born of the spirit is spirit." This is our second birth, our spiritual birth. You, your spirit, must be born again.

In John 3:5, Jesus answered, "Truly, truly, I say to you, unless one is born of water (salvation, and the Word of God) and the Spirit (being born again), he cannot enter the kingdom of God." And the Spirit means being born again or accepting Jesus Christ as your Savior.

Our **body** was *formed*, but the spirit and soul, the inner man, were created. The breath of life makes the body, soul, and spirit live and function together. When the believer dies, his body is buried. The believer's soul and spirit will go to Heaven and be with God until he is reunited with his soul and spirit again at the Rapture. At the Rapture, the Saints, the believer's eternal being, will be made whole in body, soul, and spirit, capable of living an eternal life (1 Corinthians 15:51-58; Philippians 3:21; Romans 8:18-25).

When an unbeliever dies, the body is also buried. The unbeliever's soul and spirit will go to Hell to be tormented until it is reunited again with the unbeliever's body, soul, and spirit at the Great White Throne Judgment, before being thrown into the Lake of Fire (Revelation 20:11-15). We will learn more about the Great White Throne Judgment and the Lake of Fire later.

What Kind of Bodies Will We Have in Heaven?

The bodies that the believers have on this earth now can perish and decay, they are mortal bodies, and a mortal body is not suitable for eternal life.

The promise from God is that we will get a new *physical* body beyond anything we can presently comprehend. 1 Corinthians 15:50-54 says our flesh and blood cannot inherit the Kingdom of God, nor does the perishable body (our earthly mortal body) inherit the imperishable (heavenly) body. This means our mortal earthly body is not capable of going to Heaven. We have to have a new heavenly or immortal body to live in Heaven.

We will have immortal, resurrected, and restored eternal bodies that will live forever. Our body in Heaven is immortal and will never decay. Our body will be imperishable, one that is enduring and lasting forever. We will have glorious and beautiful new bodies in Heaven.

The information about our resurrected physical body comes from Jesus in His forty days on earth between His resurrection when He came out of the grave to His ascension when He went to Heaven. In Luke 24:39, Jesus said, "See My hands and My feet, that it is I, Myself; touch Me and see, for a spirit does not have flesh and bones as you see that I have." Jesus is saying He is not a spirit. Jesus went into the grave and came out the same, except in a resurrected body fit for Heaven. We know from scripture that Jesus also ate on two different occasions in His resurrected body during the forty days (John 20:27).

Jesus was recognized in His resurrected body. We will also be recognized in Heaven and recognize each other. Do not be worried, our past will not be recognizable. Our spirits will be renewed, and sin will be forgotten. Just for your reassurance, everyone will only remember the good. All tears will be wiped away, and no more crying will occur. Remember, you are the Bride of Christ in Heaven.

1 Corinthians 15:39-42 states, "All flesh is not the same flesh. There is one flesh of man, another flesh of animals, another flesh of birds, and another of fish. There are also heavenly bodies and earthly bodies, but the glory of the heavenly body is different from the earthly body. There is the glory of the sun and another glory of the moon, and another glory of the stars. Also, the resurrection of the dead, which is buried, is perishable. It is raised imperishable and cannot be a destroyed body. The body dies in

dishonor, and it is raised in <u>glory</u>. The body is buried or dies in weakness and is raised in power. It died a natural body and raised a resurrected spiritual body." A Glorified body means transforming from our earthly body into an immortal body that can live in Heaven forever. This means uniting the dead body with its soul and spirit. To restore the dead to life in glorification, to life in a body fit for Heaven.

Believers will have an incorruptible body with no aging. The body will be beautiful, glorious, powerful, perfect in every way, and one that can spiritually travel. The body will never get physically tired again (1 Corinthians 15:41-43).

In the Book of Revelation, Jesus is speaking to the churches. He tells them that everyone will get a new name in Heaven in addition to a new body. Revelation 2:17 states, "To him who overcomes (saved and going to Heaven), to him I will give some of the hidden manna, the bread of life, and I will give him a white stone, and a new name written on the stone which no one knows but he who receives it." We will get a new name along with a new resurrected body in Heaven.

Since we know about Heaven and Eternity. It is also important that we understand what Hell is and what it is like.

Chapter Four

◇◇◇◇

WHAT IS HELL?

HELL IS NOT a good place. It is void of anything good. It is a place of constant torment, burning with fire and brimstone.

Even though Hell is described using terminologies such as fire and flames, it is not meant to be thought of as only a physical burning place. Hell is described as a place of torment. The worst aspect of Hell is an Eternity of conscious, guilty, shameful separation from God and all forms of goodness. In that sense, Hell is far worse than a literal inferno or fire.

Fire is often used as a symbol of God's judgment. The symbolism stems from God's use of fire to punish the wicked. The Lord rained down fire and brimstone on the cities of Sodom and Gomorrah as punishment for their wickedness in Genesis 19:24 and for the destruction of Elijah's enemies in 2 Kings 1:12. The prophets often described God with a stream of fire coming from His throne, a symbol of His Holy punishment of sin.

We do not know the actual location of Hell. The Bible refers to the pit or the depths of the lower parts of the earth. But be assured that God knows where it is.

Sheol and Hades

The Old Testament teaches that there is life after death, and all wicked people went to a place of conscious existence called Sheol. The Hebrew word for Hell is *Sheol*, Sheol is also known as the "pit." *Hades* is the Greek word for Hell. Hades means "unseen." Sheol, Hades, and Hell are the same place and in the same place. Luke 16:19-31 describes this place as a realm, an abode, a domain, and a place of activity. The dwelling place beneath the earth for the unredeemed dead or the spirits of the damned.

In the <u>Old Testament</u>, when a believer or an unbeliever died, they went to Abraham's bosom or Hades. There were two divisions or two compartments there. One compartment held the believers, and the other side or compartment held the unbelievers. It was a place of blessing and comfort and a place of judgment.

The dwelling place for the believers was a place of comfort called Abraham's bosom and Paradise. Abraham's bosom was considered a place of rest, contentment, and peace. It was called Abraham's bosom because Abraham was the father of the Jews and the father of many nations, both Jews and Gentiles. The other compartment for the unbeliever is a place of judgment and torment.

Luke 16:26 states that the two compartments were separated by a great chasm that could not be crossed. Luke tells the story of the poor man (meaning helpless) and the rich man and what happened to them when they died. Lazarus, the poor or helpless man went to Abraham's bosom, the place of comfort, and the unrighteous rich man went to Hades the place of torment.

The believer and the unbeliever stayed on their separate sides of the chasm until Jesus died on the cross and paid for our sins.

On the cross, after Jesus said, "It is finished," he bowed his head and gave up His spirit (John 19:30). His body was taken off the cross and placed in a tomb for three days (John 19-40-42). He died in the flesh and was placed in the tomb, but He did not die in the spirit. His spirit went below to the judgment side of Hades where the unbelievers are. There, Jesus took every sin that man could ever comment and took the sin upon himself and paid the price for our sins in Hades.

Ephesians 4:8-10 states Jesus descended into the lower parts of the earth. Jesus did not ascend or leave until He had taken our sin upon himself in Hades.

After paying the price for our sin in the judgment side of Hades, Jesus went across the chasm to the believers' side in Abraham's bosom. By the

Holy Spirit's anointing, Jesus preached to the spirits in prison, to the ones on the unbeliever's side (1 Peter 3:18-19).

Jesus then gathered all the believers in Abraham's bosom and ascended with them to Heaven up above the earth where the present Heaven is today. Abraham's bosom is now empty, but the judgment side of Hades is not empty. It is still there with unbelievers in it. They have not been moved, that is where the unbelievers go today when they die, Hades/Hell. In Luke 23:42-43, the criminal next to Jesus on the cross said to Jesus, "Jesus, remember me when you come in Your kingdom!" I believe the criminal was referring to Jesus' Millennial Kingdom. In Luke 23:43, Jesus replied to the criminal, "Truly I say to you, today you shall be with me in Paradise." What did Jesus mean in Paradise today? Jesus knew the criminal believed in Him, and the criminal would not have to wait until Jesus' Kingdom. When the criminal died on the cross, he went down to Abraham's bosom to Paradise. When Jesus ascended and lead a host of captives (the believers) from Abraham's bosom to Heaven is when the criminal also went to Heaven (Ephesians 4:8).

Gehenna

When Jesus talked to the people and to His disciples, He gave them warnings of the consequences of sin and of Hell. They related to Hell as a place they knew as Gehenna. The Valley of Gehenna was an actual place adjacent to the old city of Jerusalem. Gehenna comes from the Old Testament Hebrew word *Hinnom*, then translated into the Greek word Gehenna meaning Hell. The Valley of Gehenna ran from the Jaffa Gate on the west side of the Old City of Jerusalem, then ran along the south side, going eastward until it met and dumped into the Kidron Valley.

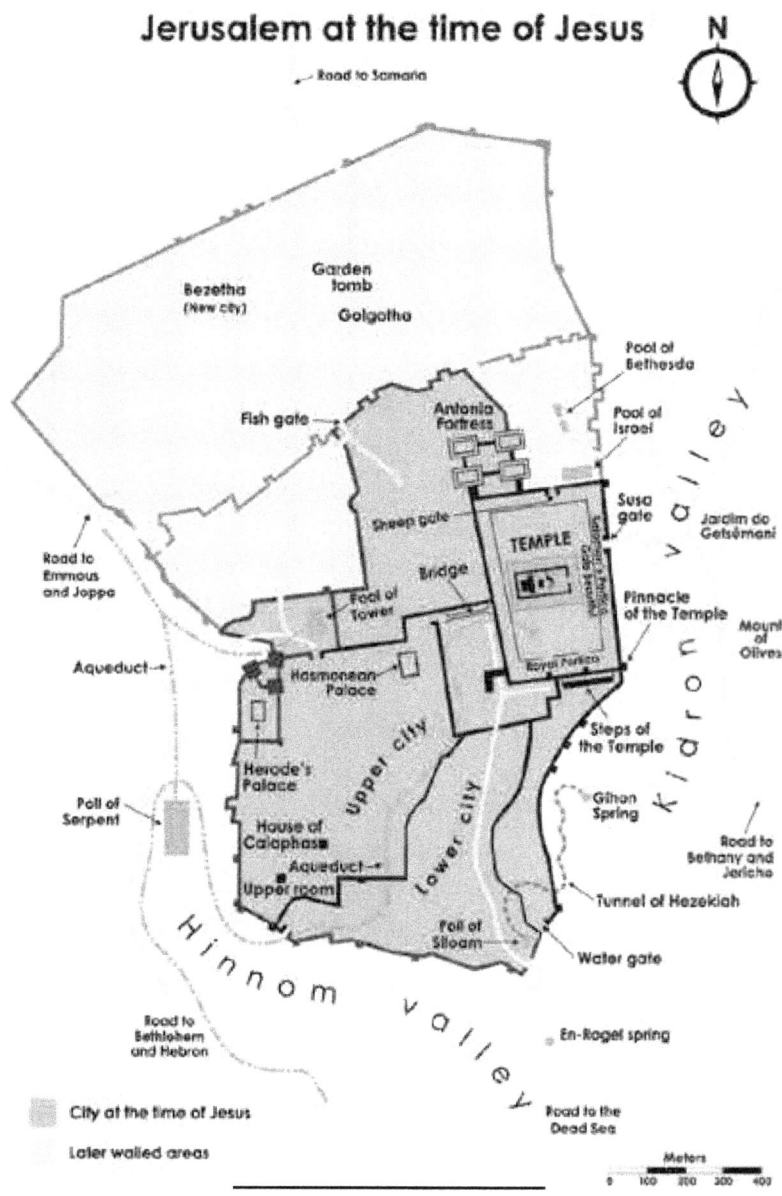

Jerusalem at the time of Jesus

This map shows where the Hinnom Valley was located and where it meets the Kidron Valley

Gehenna was a refuse heap, a ditch for the city dump, the place where the people of Jerusalem tossed their garbage and waste. It was a deep, narrow valley to the southern outer edge of Jerusalem. Gehenna became the common cesspool of the city of Jerusalem into which its sewage and all its solid fifth were collected and carried off by the waters of the Kidron Valley. There was a constantly burning fire to consume the trash. This last stop in Gehenna was for all items judged by men to be worthless.

This deep, constantly-burning Valley of Gehenna was known as "the place down there in the valley." Dead animals, the bodies of executed criminals, and the wicked who were considered undeserving and denied a decent burial would eventually be cast into the flames to burn in Gehenna. Sulfur would be added to assist in the burning, which produces an acrid odor. Brimstone is the biblical name for sulfur. Wild animals and dogs would fight along the heap's edges over the food scraps and make <u>gnashing sounds with their teeth</u>.

The people of Jesus' time related the word Hell to Gehenna. It served as a receptacle of all sorts of putrefying matter and all that defiled the Holy City, Jerusalem. It became the place of everlasting punishment and its ever-burning fires and the smell of sulfur.

The Bible gives several references to the gnashing of teeth and Hell. "Those who commit lawlessness (evil) Jesus will cast the unbelievers into the furnace, the Lake of Fire; in that place, there shall be weeping and gashing of teeth (Matthew 13:41-42).

"And I say to you, that many shall come from east and west, and recline at the table with Abraham, and Isaac, and Jacob, in the kingdom of Heaven; but to the sons of the kingdom (unrepentant Jews) shall be cast out into the outer darkness, in that place, there shall be weeping and gnashing of teeth" (Matthew 8:11-12). "Jesus will say, I tell you, I do not know where you are from; Depart from Me, all you evildoers. There will be weeping and gnashing of teeth there when you are cast out" (Luke 13:27-28).

Who Goes to Hell?

There is a difference between unbelievers, nonbelievers, and disbelievers. They could all be considered the same, but there is a little difference between them.

1. The *un-believer* rejects Christ or does not believe in Christ as his personal Savior or refuses to believe in a Deity. An unbeliever lacks faith in any religion. If a person is not a believer, that is, if they do not believe in something, they are an unbeliever. They are a doubter or a skeptic. Unbelief forms moral resistance to God.

2. The *non-believer* is a person who does not believe in any religious faith, especially in God. He wants an object for his faith. A non-believer is called a heathen, idolater, or pagan.

3. The *dis-believer* is someone who denies the existence of God. An atheist is someone that does not believe in any god or deity.

People make their own decisions concerning their eternal destiny in Heaven or Hell. The decision to go to Hell is totally up to each person. No one makes a person go to Hell. A person sends himself to Hell by his own free will, actions, and decision. People who do not accept or acknowledge Jesus Christ as their Lord and Savior will go to Hell.

In the same way, it is a person's own decision if they accept Jesus and thus go to Heaven. No one makes a person go to Heaven. In John 14:6, Jesus answered, "I am the way and the truth and the life. No one comes to the Father except through me." Salvation is through Jesus Christ.

Hell or Heaven, the decision is yours to make

1 Corinthians 6:9-10 specifically tells us who will go to Hell. The scriptures say do not be deceived by not believing who will go to Hell. They are:

1. The unrighteous and the wicked.
2. The fornicators.
3. Idolaters, who idol something other than God.
4. The adulterers.
5. The effeminate or homosexual.
6. The thieves.
7. The covetous, those that want what someone else has.
8. The drunkards.
9. The revilers that speak abusively to others.
10. The swindlers that deceive others.

Hell is where the unbelievers are held, it is not the unbeliever's final destination for eternal life. Hell is a temporary or holding place for all those waiting until their final resurrection and judgment. The spiritually dead in Hell are those without God and will go to the Lake of Fire for their Eternity.

The Lake of Fire

Hell, and the Lake of Fire are two different places. Hell is where the wicked, the sinner, the unsaved, and the abominable go when they die. The Lake of Fire is the unbeliever's final destination, their Eternity. When unbelievers die, they go to Hell. They will remain in Hell until Hell is emptied at the end of the Millennium. Their soul and spirit will be physically resurrected from Hell and united with their body. They will individually stand before God at the Great White Throne Judgment. Revelation 20:13-15 tells us the books will be opened at the Great White Throne Judgment, and those in Hell will be sentenced to life in the Lake of Fire.

Revelation 19:20 states they are thrown alive into the Lake of Fire that burns with brimstone. Revelation 20:10 continues, "And the devil who deceived them was thrown into the lake of fire and brimstone where the beast (antichrist) and the false prophet already are, and they will be tormented day and night forever and ever."

The Lake of Fire is the place of eternal torment for all the unrepentant wicked, both human and angelic. Satan and his fallen angels will also be in the Lake of Fire. It is described as a place of burning sulfur, and those in it will experience the eternal, unspeakable agony of unrelenting torment. They will not be tortured but will be constantly tormented. Those who have rejected Christ and are in the temporary abode of the dead in Hell have as their final destination the Lake of Fire.

Matthew 25:41 tells us that the Lake of Fire is prepared for spiritual beings, the devil, and Satan's angels. "Depart from me, you cursed ones into eternal fire, He prepared for Satan and his angels." No man needs to go there, but if he persists in serving Satan, he will have to spend Eternity with Satan in the Lake of Fire.

Revelation 21:8 explicitly tells who will be in the Lake of Fire.

1. The cowardly: those who will not turn from their wicked ways.
2. The unbelieving: the spiritually lost, and not saved.

3. The abominable: the bad, unpleasant, and disgusting.

4. The murderers.

5. The whoremongers: those who have dealings with prostitutes.

6. The sorcerers: those that claim to have magic powers.

7. Idolaters: those who worship something other than God.

8. All liars.

These shall have their part in the Lake of Fire, which is the **second death**. They died first and went to Hell. They die the second time, explained as the second separation from God, and will go to the Lake of Fire.

Revelation 20:15 tells us, "If anyone's name was not found written in the *Book of Life*, he was thrown into the lake of fire." The wicked sinner will go from Hell to the Lake of Fire.

We reviewed Heaven, Hell, and the Lake of Fire. Now, let us explore more events that will take place for the believer in the Afterlife. One of the first events that start the believer's Afterlife is the Rapture.

Chapter Five

◇◇◇◇

THE RAPTURE

THE WORD RAPTURE does not appear in the Bible, it is taken from the Latin word *Rapio*, meaning to seize or snatch up. The Greek word for Rapture is *Harpaso*, meaning to snatch up suddenly and decisively.

The Rapture is a Biblical event for born-again believers who have salvation through Jesus Christ. To be Raptured means to leave this earth and be caught up to meet Jesus <u>in the air</u> and go to Heaven. Believers who have died and are buried in their graves, and all living believers at the Rapture will go to Heaven.

The Rapture of the Church from earth to Heaven is in 1 Thessalonians 4:17. "Then we who are alive and remain shall be caught up together (Raptured, *Rapio, Harpaso*) with them (in the graves) in the clouds to meet the Lord in the air, and thus we shall always be with the Lord."

The purpose of the Rapture is for Jesus to take the Saints to Heaven to be with Him. Only the physical body goes into the grave when our earthly body dies. The soul and spirit of all believers go to Heaven to be with God. The soul and spirit are waiting in Heaven until Jesus comes to resurrect the body from the grave, restoring the dead to life. The souls and spirits will come with Jesus to reunite with the bodies (from the graves) to be resurrected into a glorified state. Glorified means transforming from our lowly earthly bodies into bodies that can live forever, to the glory fitted for Christ. This is the same glorified body that Jesus has in Heaven.

The Rapture's primary purpose is to protect the Saints of Jesus, His people, so they will escape the wrath of the Tribulation. Christ will not let, His Saints, His Bride become a battered and assaulted Bride that goes through the Tribulation.

Most of the descriptions of the Rapture come from the writings of the Apostle Paul. Paul writes to the Corinthians in 1 Thessalonians 4:15-18. "For this, we say to you by the word of the Lord, that we, (the believers) who are alive and remain (on the earth) until the coming of the Lord (caught up, raptured) shall not precede (or go before) those that have fallen asleep (died and are in their graves). For the Lord, Himself will descend, (come down) from Heaven with a <u>shout</u>, with the voice of the archangel, and with the trumpet (the shofar), of God, and the dead in Christ (those in their graves), shall rise *first*. Then we who are alive and shall remain (the believers alive on earth) will be caught up together with them (the ones in the graves) <u>in the clouds</u> to meet the Lord <u>in the air</u>; thus, we shall always be with the Lord."

Luke 9:27 continues, "I say to you truthfully, there are some of those standing here (on the earth) who shall not taste death until they see the kingdom of God." Never tasting death means they will not die a physical death on this earth. They will be alive when they go in the Rapture to Heaven.

Apostle Paul tells the Corinthians in 1 Corinthians 15:50, "Now I say this, brethren, that flesh and blood cannot inherit the kingdom of God; nor does the perishable inherit the imperishable. Behold, I tell you a *mystery*; we shall not all die (a physical death on earth), but we shall all be changed, in a moment, in the twinkling of an eye (instantaneous) at the last trumpet (shofar); for the trumpet (shofar) will sound, and the dead (in the graves) will be raised imperishable, and we shall be changed. For this perishable must put on the imperishable, and this mortal human must put on immortality." Immortality means to have an unending existence. A state of endless life beyond the power of death, which is obtained following the resurrection, the rising from the dead.

Apostle Paul tells us some essential information about the flesh and blood of a human. A human cannot enter on their own merit. Humans will enter Heaven through their salvation in Jesus Christ. Their flesh and blood will be changed into glorified bodies, then they can enter God's Kingdom. Paul is saying our human body is perishable, it can decay, and our human body must be laid aside before we can enter Heaven. A glorified body means to be transformed from our earthly body into an immortal nondecaying body that can live forever in Heaven, Millennial Kingdom and Eternity.

There will be at least two sounds made by the shofar, for the Rapture. The Rapture will start at the *first sound* of the trumpet, for the dead in their graves to be raised spiritually to meet Jesus <u>in the air</u>. At the *last trumpet*, the living will be changed spiritually and be caught up with the dead from their graves to meet the Lord <u>in the air</u>. In a moment, in the twinkling of an eye at the *last trumpet*, the living believer shall be changed, and all go together to Heaven (1 Corinthians 15:52).

In 2 Thessalonians 2:6-8, it states, "And you know <u>what restrains Satan now</u>, so that in Satan's time he may be revealed. For the mystery of lawlessness (evil) is already at work; only He (the Holy Spirit) who now restrains will do until He (the Holy Spirit and the Church) is taken out of the way (Rapture). And then that lawless one (Satan) will be revealed whom the Lord will slay with the breath of His mouth (the Word of God) and bring to an end, by the appearance of His Second Coming." The Church, and the Holy Spirit, are hindering Satan today. The Body of Christ, the believers, must be taken out of the world (Rapture) and go to Heaven so God can permit and allow Satan to appear and the Tribulation to take place.

The Shofar

Another name for the trumpet in the Bible is the shofar. The shofar is a ram's horn or kudu antelope horn and symbolizes God's voice. The shofar is a representative of the prophets, who called upon the Jewish people to become better in the service of God.

The shofar comes from the Kudu Antelope.

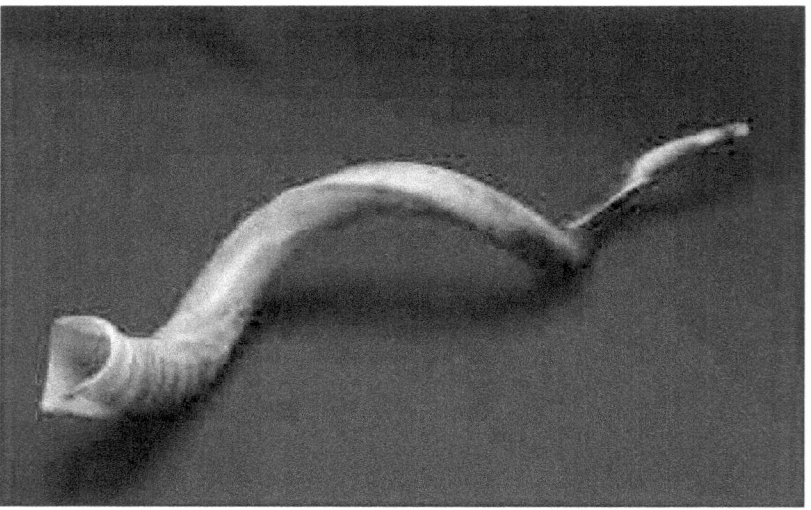

The Shofar

In the Old Testament, a shofar was used as a <u>signaling device</u>, as shown in this scripture. "When you blow an alarm (a shofar), the camps that are on the east side <u>shall set out</u> (start, move)" (Numbers 12:5).

In battle, the shofar signaled the warriors and sent God's voice out. "And when you go to <u>war</u> in your land against the adversary who attacks you, then you shall <u>sound an alarm</u> (God's voice), with the trumpets, that you may be remembered before the Lord your God, and you shall be saved from your enemies" (Numbers 10:9).

"So, Joab blew the trumpet, and all the people halted and pursued Israel no longer, nor did they continue to fight anymore" (2 Samuel 2:28). This scripture tells us the shofar is sounded, God's voice is heard, and the enemy does not fight Israel anymore.

The dead sea scrolls describe the priest carrying the shofar to stand in the gap between the regiments of the Israelites. The High Priest would go first onto the battlefield, armed only with the shofar that preceded the Ark of the Covenant. The continuous blowing of the shofar brought down the walls of Jericho. "Take up the ark of the covenant and let seven priests bear seven trumpets of *rams' horns* (shofar) before the ark; then on the seventh day you shall march around the city seven times, and the priest shall blow the trumpets/shofars" (Joshua 6:4).

The Lord brought the Hebrews out of Egypt and spoke to them through the shofar's sound. In Revelation, when John heard the voice of the Lord, he heard it as the sound of a shofar. This was part of the history and heritage of the people living in Apostle John's time, hearing the Word of the Lord from and through the shofar. John knew what it meant, and it certainly got his attention.

John heard God's voice as the sound of the trumpet, the shofar. "I, John, was in the Spirit on the Lord's Day, and I heard behind me a loud voice like a trumpet" (Revelation 1:10).

John heard from God with the sound of the trumpet or shofar several times in the Book of Revelation. "After this, I looked and behold, a door standing open in heaven! And the first voice, which I, John, had heard speaking to me was like a trumpet, and said, Come up here, and I will show you what must take place after this" (Revelation 4:1). John heard God's voice in the blowing of the shofar.

My husband has studied the shofar and the sounds of the shofar for many years. Besides studying the Bible, he uses the Hebrew oral laws, called the Mishna. He also studied what the Rabbis had to say about the shofar in his research. My husband has been given the gift of blowing the shofar. He blows a kosher Yemenite shofar from the Kudu antelope that he bought in Israel. A shofar is constructed of soft bone tissues covered by an outer layer of keratin, the same material as fingernails. In order for the shofar to be kosher the inner tissue layer must be removed. This is accomplished by drying the horn for about a year.

He blew the shofar over the Valley of Elah, where David fought Goliath. He has blown the shofar at funerals and at several Christian functions in our city. He blows the shofar for the beginning of many of our church groups ushering in God's voice.

Another interesting fact that my husband found in his study, is that the cockcrow refers to the shofar in scripture, not a cock or a rooster. Matthew 26:34 (KJV) "Verily I say unto thee (Peter), that this night, before the cock crow, thou shalt deny me thrice."

The cockcrow was the name or the nickname referring to the time of the watch or duty of the watchman from midnight to the 3 a.m. Jesus would have known this time as the cockcrow. Jesus wasn't waiting for a roster to crow. Jesus knew exactly the time the cockcrow or the shofar would sound. The Priest would sound the shofar from the trumpeting stone for the change of the watchmen, and Jesus would have known this. Jesus told Peter he would deny Him before the 3 a.m. watch when the shofar would be blown.

The Priest would sound the shofar from the Trumpeting Stone, which is the pinnacle stone or the highest stone on the southwest corner of the temple mount. The Trumpeting Stone overlooked the city of David, and poultry was not allowed in the city limits, according to some Rabbis.

The shofar was how the watchman would alert the people of approaching danger and also the shift change of the watchman. It was like a clock for the people. "And I set the watchmen over you, saying, listen to the sound of the trumpet!" (Jeremiah 6:17).

There is a name and a reason for each sound the shofar makes. Each sound meant something to the people of Jesus' time.

"You shall then sound the ram's horn abroad on the tenth day of the seventh month; on the day of atonement, you shall sound a horn all through your land" (Leviticus 25:9).

"Blow a trumpet in Zion, and sound an alarm on My holy mountain! Let all the inhabitants of the land tremble, for the day of the Lord is coming; surely it is near" (Joel 2:1).

The shofar is the Jubilee trumpet (freedom), the sounding of liberty. Today the shofar is to Israel as the Liberty Bell is to America, representing liberty and freedom.

The shofar is God's voice that will call us up in the Rapture. "In a moment, in the twinkling of an eye, at the last trumpet (shofar); for the trumpet (shofar) will sound, and the dead will be raised imperishable, and we shall be changed" (1 Corinthians 15:52).

Rapture Versus the Second Coming of Christ

The Rapture and the Second Coming of Jesus are two different events at two different times. The Rapture is first and takes place *before* the seven years of the Tribulation start. The Second Coming is at the end of the seven years of Tribulation. These two events will take place seven years apart.

At the Second Coming of Christ, Jesus comes to the earth with His Bride, the believers, the Saints who have been in Heaven with Him. The Second Coming is when Jesus comes to the earth to live and fulfill His mission in the Millennial Kingdom.

1. The Rapture occurs before the Tribulation. The Second Coming ends the Tribulation.

2. At the Rapture, Jesus comes for His Saints. At the Second Coming, Jesus comes with His Saints.

3. In the Rapture, Jesus meets His Saints in the air. At the Second Coming, Jesus and His Saints return to the earth together.

4. The Rapture is imminent, at any moment, with no signs. At the Second Coming, there are definite predicted signs that occur before Jesus arrives.

5. The Rapture is for the believers in an instant. At the Second Coming, the Armageddon War is raging, and everyone will see.

6. The Rapture comes before the Day of Wrath. The Second Coming concludes the Day of Wrath.

7. In the Rapture, there is no reference to Satan. At the Second Coming, Satan is bound for one thousand years.

The Unbelievers Left on Earth

All the believers in Jesus will be removed from the earth by the Rapture. This will leave only the unbelievers to enter the seven years of the Tribulation and continue to live on this earth.

People will be shocked by the mysterious evacuation of millions of people. The Rapture will leave its mark on humankind and the earth itself. What will happen when the believers driving in their cars, the airline pilots, train engineers, and those operating moving equipment are suddenly snatched from the controls of their moving vehicles? The Rapture will leave a vacancy of many people on this earth. This will cause the most chaotic and disruptive consequences that any single event has ever created. The common denominator of those left on earth will be their unbelief in Jesus Christ. Anyone left on the earth after the Rapture is an unbeliever, and they will enter the Tribulation.

Even if an unbeliever becomes a believer the day after the Rapture, it will be too late for that person to go in the Rapture, but not too late for that person to be saved.

When the Rapture takes place, the world and the media will have many scenarios and reasons why the people have left or been taken away. They will justify the absence of the believers, and the people left behind will believe Satan's lies and accept the world's excuses.

Chapter Six

◇◇◇◇

THE JUDGMENT SEAT OF CHRIST

THE JUDGMENT SEAT of Christ is not to be confused with The Great White Throne Judgment. These two events are at two different times and in two separate locations. The Judgment Seat of Christ is for the believers and takes place in Heaven. The Great White Throne Judgment is for the *unbelievers* who have been held in Hell. This judgment takes place at the end of the Millennium. We will learn about the Millennium later in the book.

The Judgment Seat of Christ is one of the first events that will take place for believers upon entering Heaven. Each believer will stand individually before the Judgment Seat of Christ. This judgment has nothing to do with salvation because only the saved will be in Heaven. This will not be a judgment of the believer's sins because sins were forgiven and wiped away when salvation through Jesus Christ is chosen before entering Heaven.

"For we shall all stand before God's judgment seat. So then, each of us will give an account of himself to God" (Romans 14:10-12). The Judgment Seat of Christ is when all believers will give an account of what they did while on earth to serve Jesus and to further the Gospel of Jesus Christ.

What we desire to hear is, "Well done, good and faithful servant" (Matthew 25:2).

Storing Up Our Treasures in Heaven

Let us continue to learn more about the Judgement Seat of Christ. Matthew 6:19-21 tells us, "Do not lay up for yourselves treasures upon earth where moth and rust destroy and where thieves break in and steal, but where your treasure is, there will your heart be also."

We are encouraged to store our treasures in Heaven instead of storing our treasures on this earth. What do treasures mean exactly? Treasures refer to our deeds, our work for the Kingdom of God. What we do to further the Gospel and the Body of Christ. What we do to help others come to know who Jesus is, the souls we win for Jesus, and what acts of service we do in church and community groups. Some Jewish people define storing up treasures in Heaven as deeds of mercy and kindness to people in distress.

Treasures on earth are temporary, materialistic, and limited. The way to store our treasures in Heaven is to invest in something that will go to Heaven. We should invest in people because we want them to go to Heaven.

Our life on this earth is short compared to our everlasting life. We only have one chance at life, and we will be held accountable for it. What we do for Christ in this life will also make a difference in our serving positions in the Millennial Kingdom, which I will discuss later.

Our Rewards

"We must all appear before the Judgment Seat of Christ that each one may be recompensed or reimbursed for his deeds in the body of Christ according to what he has done whether good or bad" (2 Corinthians 5:10). Standing before the Judgment Seat of Christ involves believers giving an account of how they served Christ and advanced the Kingdom of God while on the earth.

Good deeds or works have *nothing* to do with receiving salvation. Salvation is through Jesus Christ. You cannot work your way into Heaven.

Good deeds and works are actions that promote and further the Gospel, the Body of Christ.

Bad deeds or bad works are not sins but are described as worthless or unrewardable deeds. Bad can mean good deeds or works done with the wrong motive or for oneself. God knows an individual's heart and knows their motives. "The Lord will bring the things hidden in darkness and disclose the motives of men's hearts" (1 Corinthians 4:5). When our motives and the things we do for the Lord are pure, so are our deeds and works for Him.

"Each man's work will become evident; for the day will show it (Judgment Seat of Christ) because it (deeds and works) is to be revealed with fire (judgment); and the fire itself will test the quality of each man's work. If any man's work which he has built upon it remains, he shall receive a reward. If any man's work is burned up, he shall suffer loss (no reward); but <u>he himself shall be saved</u>" (1 Corinthians 3:13-15).

Salvation is a gift, but rewards are earned. The quality of our service is the principle or standard by which something will be judged or decided. If any man's work on earth is built for Jesus, that reward will be there when he gets to Heaven. If we start witnessing to a person, and if someone else builds upon it, that person will also receive a reward as well.

All believers will stand before the Judgment Seat of Christ in Heaven. Each believer will be individually judged in a review of their deeds and works that they did on earth for Christ's Kingdom. As scripture states, each man's deeds and works will become evident and will be revealed by fire and purification. Fire symbolizes the Holiness of God and His judgments. Purification means the removal or extraction of our bad deeds and works. Fire is God's judgment, and purification is cleansing or removing. Everything bad and all worthless work will be burned up or removed. In other words, all of our good deeds and works for Christ and His Kingdom will be <u>revealed</u>, and all of our bad deeds and works will be <u>removed</u> at the Judgment Seat of Christ.

In Revelation 22:12, Jesus says, "Behold, I am coming quickly, and My reward is with Me, to render to every man according to what he has done." Our rewards will make a difference in our serving positions during the Millennial Kingdom, where we will rule and reign with Jesus for one thousand years.

There is a difference between rewards and crowns. Both are revealed at the Judgment Seat of Christ.

Our Crowns

The Greek word for judgment is *bēma*. There was a judgment seat or a *bēma* seat in the marketplace of every major city in ancient times. A Roman magistrate or ruler would sit on a raised *bēma* seat where the ruler would make decisions and pass out sentences to the people (Matthew 27:19; John 19:13).

Apostle Paul's use of sports metaphors is prevalent throughout his letters to the Corinthians, Galatians, Ephesians, and Philippians. Paul adds sports imagery for those who observed and perhaps even participated in the Greek Olympic games. At the Greek Olympic games, the winner, or the victors as they were called, received no medals. Instead, they received crowns made from olive branches and leaves from the sacred olive tree. The participant who finished in first place received a crown as he personified or embodied the Greek concept of excellence. The judge of the Olympic games sat in a special area on an elevated platform known as the *bēma* seat in the Olympic stadium. The winners, the victors, would go to the *bēma* seat to receive the winner's crown of victory from the judges. The believer's faithful service to Jesus will be evaluated, and they will receive their *rewards* and *crowns*. James 1:12 is a good review of how we should understand the Judgment Seat of Christ. "Blessed is a man who perseveres under trial or trouble; for once he has been approved, he will receive the *crown of life*, which the Lord has promised to those who love Him."

There are five *crowns* listed in the Bible that a believer may receive. A believer may also receive more than one crown at the Judgment Seat of Christ.

1. The *Victor's* Crown is the Incorruptible, Imperishable Crown. It is the self-discipline required to do God's work on earth. It takes self- discipline to run the race with the Lord (1 Corinthians 9:25-27).

2. The *Crown of Joy or Rejoicing* is for those speaking, teaching, and proclaiming the gospel of salvation, bringing others to know Christ. This crown is often called the Soul-Winner's Crown (1 Thessalonians 2:19).

3. The *Crown of Righteousness* is learning the Word of God, the doers of the Word. Those learning, living, and teaching the Word of God. This crown is for those who long for Heaven, their true home. It is for those who long to see Jesus. Those who are waiting and longing for the Lord to return (2 Timothy 4:1-8).

4. The *Crown of Life* is for those that gave their lives for Christ, the martyrs. Those who maintain, press on, persevere while under trial and suffering, and keep their love and faith for Christ (Revelation 2:10; James 1:12).

5. The *Crown of Glory* goes to those who answered the leadership call to the Body of Christ. They are the faithful servants of God. The pastors, ministers, elders, teachers, and those serving in the ministry (1 Peter 5:4).

It is difficult to say what our crowns will look like. We know the victors at the Olympic games received crowns of branches and leaves from the olive tree. Jesus wore a crown of thorns. There is a difference between a crown and a diadem. A crown is for victory, and a diadem is usually a jeweled crown for royalty or authority. There is the gold crown or diadem that represents the King's authority. No matter what crown or crowns we receive in Heaven, they will be magnificent.

Revelation 4:8-11 explains that the twenty-four elders, representing the church-age saints, fall down, lay flat before God, and worship Him. They lay their crowns before the throne, saying, "Worthy are you, our Lord." A crown will seem an insignificant gift to present to Jesus, who gave His life for us. The twenty-four elders' response is most likely how we will respond when we receive our crowns. We will be so overcome with gratitude for what Jesus has done for us that we will worship Him and lay our crowns before the throne. Although the scriptures do not specifically state this is what we will do, we will likely follow the example of the twenty-four elders in casting our crowns before Jesus.

What Will the Believers See and Do in Heaven?

It is encouraging to know that the Bible tells us our citizenship is in Heaven. "For our citizenship is in heaven, not on this earth, from which we also eagerly wait for a Savior, the Lord Jesus Christ, who will transform the body of our humble state into conformity with the body of His glory" (Philippians 3:20).

Revelation 4:3-6 gives us a glimpse of what John saw in Heaven. God is seated on His throne, surrounded by a rainbow of emerald green, representing the grace of God that brings us to Him. The twenty-four elders are seated on their thrones, representing the church-age Saints. Before the throne is a sea of glass, representing God's Holiness. The four living ones, the angelic beings, will sing praises to God, the One on the throne, and all of Heaven will worship the glorified Christ.

Our time in Heaven will be vastly superior to our lives on earth. We become absent from our bodies and become present with the Lord. We will not be angels, but we will be with angels in the presence of God's Holiness. We will embrace God's justice and righteousness (2 Corinthians 5:8).

If you have ever longed to give all of yourself in worship, there will be an abundance of praise and worship in Heaven. We will have the most beautiful praise and worship we have ever known, with many sounds of instruments for music. It will be glorious!

Praise is defined as a reverent feeling or showing deep and solemn respect, having great awe, love, and devotion to our Lord. Praise is to feel deep respect or admiration by extending our hands, confessing and giving our love, being thankful, and weeping before our Lord. To rave, to celebrate, and to make a show of boast.

Worship or Worthship is to honor with extravagant love and with extreme submission to God. As to when we bow down, crouch, kneel, or stoop before the Lord. The Greek states it is to kiss His master's hand, to prostrate oneself in reverence and adoration in worship.

"Oh come, let us worship and bow down; let us kneel before the Lord" (Psalm 95:6). "God is spirit, and those who worship Him must worship in spirit and truth" (John 4:24).

In Revelation 5:11-12, John looked and heard around the throne many angels, thousands and thousands of them, saying with a loud voice. "Worthy is the Lamb who was slain to receive power, wealth, wisdom, might, honor, glory, and blessing." John heard, "Every created thing which is in

Heaven and on the earth and under the earth and on the sea and all that is in them. To Him who sits on the throne and to the Lamb, be blessing and honor and glory and might forever and ever" (Revelation 5:13).

We will have the desire and will be free to praise and worship in Heaven without any limitations or be inhibited. We will praise and worship as we have never done before.

The Bride, the Wife of Christ

Scriptures show that we, the believers, the Church is already the Bride of Christ. In the following scriptures, the Greek word for the bridegroom is *numphios*. This is meaning a newly betrothed married man.

1. John called Christ the Bridegroom in John 3:29. "He who has the bride (Church) is the bridegroom (Christ); but the friend of the Bridegroom who stands and hears Him, rejoices greatly because of the Bridegroom's voice (Christ)."

2. Jesus calls Himself the Bridegroom of Christians. Jesus said, "The attendant of the bridegroom cannot mourn as long as the bridegroom (Jesus) is with them" (Matthew 9:15; Mark 2:19; Luke 5:34-35).

3. Christians are married to Christ under the covenant of the New Testament, as Israel was married to God under the covenant of the Old Testament. "For this is my blood of the covenant which is poured out for many for the forgiveness of sin" (Matthew 26:28).

4. Jesus says, "And the spirit and the bride say come, and let the one who is thirsty come" (Revelation 22:16-17). After the ascension, when Christ went to Heaven, the believers on earth are His Bride.

5. Paul used the marriage relationship to illustrate and teach the relationship of Christ to His Church. Stating for a husband to love his wife, just as Christ also loves the Church and gave Himself up for her (Ephesians 5:25; 1 Corinthians 11:3).

In John's vision in Revelation 19:7-9, John sees and hears the heavenly multitudes praising God because the marriage supper is about to begin.

"The marriage of the Lamb has come, and His bride (believers, Saints) has made herself ready" (Revelation 19:7).

And the voice from Heaven said to John, "Write, Blessed are those who are invited to the marriage supper of the Lamb" (Revelation 19:9). Those saved through Jesus are the ones invited, and they will be part of the marriage supper. Our time in Heaven will be preparation time or getting ready for the marriage supper. The marriage supper of the Lamb takes place at the end of our time in Heaven before we return to the earth with Christ at His Second Coming.

> "One of the seven angels spoke with John saying to him. Come here, I, the angel, shall show you John, the bride, the wife of the Lamb, and the angel carried John away in the Spirit to a great and high mountain and showed *John the holy city, Jerusalem*, coming down out of heaven from God" (Revelation 21:9-10).

The angel showed John *what* the Bride, the Wife of Jesus, is. It is the *Holy City, the New Jerusalem*, in the New Heavens, on the New Earth in our Eternity. The angel says the New Jerusalem *is the Bride, the Wife of Christ*. "John saw the *holy city, new Jerusalem*, coming down out of the heaven from God, made ready as a bride adorned (beautiful) for her husband" (Revelation 21:2).

It is not just one group or denomination of people, but all who have received salvation through the grace of Jesus that are collectively Jesus' Wife in New Jerusalem. The angel pointed this out to John when he promised to show John the Bride, the Lamb's Wife, the Holy City, and the heavenly Jerusalem.

Apostle Paul taught that Old Testament Saints would not be made perfect without the New Testament Saints. "And all of these, having gained approval through their faith, did not receive what was promised (the Old Testament Saints), because God had provided something better for them so that apart from us (New Testament Saints) they (Old Testament Saints) should not be made perfect" (Hebrew 11:39-40). The Old and New Testament Saints will be *perfected* together as those who make the inhabitants of the New Jerusalem.

The Jewish Wedding

Understanding the Bride, the Wife of Christ, the "Marriage Feast," and the "Marriage Supper" is easier if we know and understand the Jewish wedding customs at the time of Jesus. You will see that the Marriage Feast and the Marriage Supper are two different occasions and at two different times in a Jewish wedding.

A Jewish wedding has three significant parts. The first part is when a man found the maiden he wanted to marry, a maiden is a young unmarried female. There was no dating at this time, so when a young man found the maiden, he wanted to be his bride, the future bridegroom, or his father would present the maiden's father with a marriage contract or proposal saying the young man wanted to marry the man's daughter. The daughter and father would look over the contract, and if they agreed to the terms of the proposed contract, then the young man or his father would be obligated to pay the price of the contract for her. This contract was signed by the father of the bride-to-be and the young man, the future bridegroom.

The young man or his father would pay a very costly price, something of great value to the future bride's father, to show the father that his daughter was worth much and also to thank the father for raising such a fine daughter. With the contract agreed upon, the maiden would come in the room and say, "I do." The future bride and bridegroom would then drink wine from the same cup, this was saying they both agreed to the marriage. This was the "Marriage Feast," the bridegroom asking and the bride accepting. The bridegroom would prepare a speech for his new bride-to-be, and in that speech, it was customary to say, "I go to prepare a place for you." This would show that in the next year of separation, the bridegroom was not abandoning the bride-to-be but preparing a place for her. Then he would leave for his father's house to prepare a place for them. The second part was the betrothal or engagement period, which usually lasted about a year. During the year of betrothal time, the bride would gather her possessions for her household, known as her bridal trousseau. Like the hope chest of our grandmother's time or the wedding showers of today. This would be the gathering of items to start the household. This betrothal time was considered the same as the bride and groom being married, but the marriage was not yet consummated.

Within the year, the bridegroom would prepare two places for him and his bride. One would be a room added to the bridegroom's father's house. This would be the bridal chamber or honeymoon suite. The other would be the house for the couple to make their home on the family land. When the bridegroom finished the bridal chamber and the house, both had to be inspected and approved by the bridegroom's father. The bride would secretively be made aware in advance that the approval was about to take place. She would gather her trousseau and her bridal maidens to be ready. When the bridegroom's father gave his approval, the bridegroom, accompanied by his groomsmen, went to the bride's parent's house at midnight. This created a candlelight parade through the streets for the bridegroom to retrieve his bride. He would give a <u>shout</u> for the bride to hear. They would all join together in the parade from the bride's parent's home to the bridegroom's father's house. The bride and bridegroom would be escorted to the bridal chamber. The groomsmen would wait outside the bridal chamber until the bridegroom reported that the marriage had been consummated. The couple would stay in the bridal chamber for seven days, while the family and friends would have festive activities celebrating the marriage. An example of this was when Jesus performed His first miracle and turned water into wine for a wedding celebration.

The third phase was after the seven days, the end of the honeymoon time. The groom would appear with his bride, and they would walk with their family and friends to the "Marriage Supper or Marriage Banquet," where everyone celebrated together with the bride and groom. After the "Marriage Supper," the groom and his bride would depart for the house the groom had built for them. "For this cause, a man shall leave his father and his mother, and shall cleave to his wife; and they shall become one flesh" (Genesis 2:24; Matthew 19:5; Ephesians 5:31).

Let us see how the Jewish wedding traditions of Jesus' time relate to us. The first phase of the engagement time has already taken place for the believer. The first phase is salvation and the "Marriage Feast," when the believer says "I do" and places his faith in Jesus Christ as his Savior.

God paid the price of the contract for us through the costly blood of Jesus Christ. We are worth so much to God that He would give His only son to pay the price for us on the cross. The Church today is betrothed and engaged to Christ, and the believer is the Bride of Christ. All believers should be waiting and watching for the bridegroom's return, the Rapture. The second phase is the Rapture of the believer when Christ comes with a shout to claim His Bride. Jesus will take the believers to His Father's house in Heaven, where the believers stay for seven years. In John 14:2-4, Jesus tells us, "In My Father's house are many dwelling places; for I go to prepare a place for you. And if I go and prepare a place for you, I will come again and receive you to Myself."

The third phase is the "Marriage Supper." At the end of the seven years in Heaven will be the "Marriage Supper" of the Lamb. This represents the union between Christ and the Church (Ephesians 5:27; Revelation 19:9).

The invitation of Jesus for the people to be saved is the "Marriage Feast" (Matthew 21:1-14). "Behold I stand at the door and knock, if anyone hears My voice and opens the door, I will come into him and will dine, feast, with him, and he with Me (Revelation 3:20). The "Marriage Feast" is our salvation when we say "I do" and we accept Jesus as our Savior.

The "Marriage Supper" is at the end of the seven years in Heaven. "Blessed are those who are invited (marriage feast) and who attend (the saved) the marriage supper of the Lamb" (Revelation 19:9). The "Marriage Supper," the banquet of Jesus, is a glorious celebration for all who are invited and accept the invitation of Jesus into their hearts for salvation.

The "Marriage Supper" of the Lamb is the completion of the union between Christ and the Church (believers, Saints) (Ephesians 5:27; Revelation 19:9).

After seven years in His Father's house in Heaven and the "Marriage Supper" of the union, Jesus will take the believers (his Bride the Wife) to live with Him in His Millennial Kingdom. The believers will leave the Father's House (Heaven) and will enter Jesus' Millennial Kingdom and rule and reign with Jesus.

The Parable of the Ten Virgins

Jesus often spoke to His disciples in parables. A parable is a short simple story of comparison. When the disciples asked Jesus why He spoke in parables, Jesus told the disciples they would understand the parable, but the unbeliever would not understand it. The unbeliever could hear but not be hearing. The unbeliever could see but not be seeing. This is how we were at some time in our lives and how the unbeliever is today. The unbeliever is hearing but does not hear.

Jesus spoke to His disciples about the parable of the ten virgins. It represents the prepared believer waiting on the return of Jesus at the Rapture and the unprepared. Some will be ready, waiting, and will go with Jesus, some will be left behind.

The ten virgins took their lamps and went out to meet the bridegroom. The five wise virgins took oil in their vessels and lamps. The other five were foolish and did not take enough oil. While the bridegroom was delaying, the ten virgins fell asleep. At midnight, there was a <u>shout</u>, behold, the bridegroom is coming! Then all the virgins arose to prepare their lamps, and the foolish virgins did not have enough oil. They asked the five wise virgins for some of their oil. The wise virgins said there is not enough for both of us, so the five unprepared left to buy oil. While they were away to buy the oil, the bridegroom came. Those who were ready went with Him, and the door was closed. When the five foolish unprepared virgins returned, they said to the Lord, Lord, open to us. But the Lord answered and said to the five foolish virgins, I do not know you (Matthew 25:1-13).

Jesus is telling us that He is coming, so be ready and prepared. Do not find yourself distracted and straying from the Word of God or being caught up in the ways of this world. We could also compare this parable to the believer who has salvation in Jesus and the person who is on the fence, not knowing which way he wants to believe. He lives a good life and believes there is a Jesus but has not committed to asking Jesus for salvation. What will happen to this person when Jesus comes in the Rapture? He will be left behind.

This could also be compared to relying on someone else's knowledge of knowing the Word of God and not learning the Word for yourself. Trying to use or stand on someone else's faith and knowledge of Jesus.

The Thief in the Night

Scripture tells us that Jesus will come as a thief in the night. "But be sure of this: if the head of the house had known at what time of the night the thief was coming, he would have been on the alert and would not have allowed his house to be broken into. For this reason, you be ready too;

for the Son of Man is coming at an hour when you do not think He will" (Matthew 24:43). We will not know the hour or day, but we know Jesus is coming soon. Therefore, to the believer Jesus will not come unexpectedly.

In Revelation 16:15, Jesus says, "Behold, I am coming as a thief. Blessed is the one who stays awake and keeps his garments ready (prepared), lest he walks about naked (unprepared) and men see his shame (his unbelief)." 1 Thessalonians 5:2 says, "For you, yourselves know full well that the day of the Lord (the Rapture), will come just like a thief in the night."

These scriptures are talking to both the believer and the unbeliever, but especially to the unbeliever because they will not be saved and will be completely unprepared. Jesus will return as a thief in the night to the unbeliever, but He will not be a thief to the faithful and prepared believer. We are preparing, watching, and waiting for His glorious return in the Rapture. He says blessed is the one who stays awake, meaning prepared, for we do not know the hour or the day of our Savior's return for us.

Chapter Seven

◇◇◇◇

THE ISRAELITES

IT IS IMPORTANT to understand Israel and its descendants because they are God's chosen people, and they will be in the Tribulation, Millennium, and in Eternity.

God called the Israelites to be His chosen people, and they failed to fulfill that calling. As the seed of Abraham, the children of Israel were chosen by God to be a separate people, and holy to the Lord. God's design was for the Israelites to be a light to the Gentiles so that the Gentiles might also know God (Genesis 18:17-19; Isaiah 42:49).

A Gentile is a non-Jewish person or a person of the non-Jewish faith. The definition of the word Gentile stems from the Hebrew term goy, which means a nation, and was applied both to the Hebrews and to any other nation. The plural, *goyim*, especially with the definite article, *ha-goyim*, the nations, meant nations of the world that were not Hebrew. A Gentile can also mean a heathen, an idolater, an unbeliever, an infidel, or a pagan. The first person to be known or labeled as a Gentile was Cornelius, a Roman centurion. Christians consider him to be the first Gentile to convert to the Christian faith. Apostle Paul is considered the founder of Gentile Christianity. The two most significant figures in early Christianity are Apostle Paul and Apostle Peter. Apostle Paul took a leading role in spreading the teachings of Jesus to the Gentiles.

God's purpose for Israel from the start was to set the Israelites apart from other people by giving them His laws. He made it clear that Israel would be a special treasure to Him above all people. "For you are a holy people to the Lord your God, Who has chosen you to be a people for Himself, a special treasure above all the peoples on the face of the earth" (Deuteronomy 7:6). To *be set apart* is to be *sanctified* for holy service, or more basically, to be made holy.

God commanded Israel to be separate from other nations. This meant acting in a way different from that of the Gentiles. Leviticus 19:1 tells us, "They should be holy, set apart, for I, the Lord your God, am holy." God's purpose, the intent behind all His laws, was to create a people like Himself, a people sharing and reflecting His holiness (Genesis 1:26). Instead of the Israelites being the light to the Gentiles, the Israelites chased foreign gods and betrayed their calling to God (Hosea 11).

However, when Jesus revealed Himself as the promised King who would restore Israel (Matthew 11-12; Acts 3:19-22), He was rejected by the Jews, exactly as Isaiah had prophesied in Isaiah 52-53. Jesus, therefore, called His disciples to fulfill Abraham's commission to bless the nations (Genesis 12:2-3) by preaching the Gospel of the Kingdom to all the nations until the end of this age (Matthew 28:18-20). Apostle Paul preached the Gospel of the Kingdom to the Jews and was repeatedly rejected (Acts 13-28). Apostle Paul brought the Gospel's good news to the Gentiles. The Gentiles became Abraham's spiritual seed by faith and heirs of the promises to Abraham and his descendants (Galatians 3-4).

Jesus came, and the Gentiles were grafted into the olive tree and nourished by the root, the promises to Abraham (Ephesians 5:31). The tree, therefore, signifies the <u>collective</u> people of God. The wild branches grafted in representing the Gentile believers. The natural branches that were cut off are the Israelites and the Jews because of unbelief and idolatry. Apostle Paul compares Israel to the natural branches of a cultivated olive tree and the Gentile believers to the branches of a wild olive tree. The natural branches (Israel) were broken off, and the wild branches (Gentiles) were grafted in. The Gentiles, then, have been made partakers of the promises and inherited the blessings of God's salvation. Jewish believers remain in the tree but are joined by the Gentiles (Romans 11:17).

Romans 11 conclusively shows to the Gentile believers that God is not yet finished with Israel. Israel has only temporarily lost the privilege of representing God as His people. The gifts and calling of God cannot be changed. Therefore, Israel will be saved in order to fulfill God's covenant with Israel, including the promise of the land inheritance (Romans 11:25-28).

The natural branches of Israel were cut off because they failed God. God's purposes will not be complete until Israel is also grafted back into the people of God to share in the promises to Abraham and his seed. This brings full circle God's larger redemptive plan for both Jews and Gentiles as distinct populations of God in the Millennial Kingdom. The prophets saw this Kingdom as the final form of the olive tree so that Israel, in reversing roles, would then bless the Gentiles, enabling them to join the people of God (Zechariah 8:20-23).

These were the promises God made to the patriarchs Abraham, Isaac, and Jacob that point to modern-day Israel.

We know from the promises of the Old Testament prophecies that Israel as a nation will repent and be re-gathered to the land *in the last day* as a permanent possession. But when will the restoration of Israel take place? It has been over three thousand years since Abraham was given the promises of God. God's purpose and plan are tightly linked with Israel. When we find Israel, we will also find God. To search for Israel is to search for God, to find Israel in history is to find God there, too (Deuteronomy 30:1-10).

God appeared to Abram, whose name was later changed to Abraham, and told Abram, "Go forth from your country and from your father's house to a land that I/God will show you, and I will make you/Abram a great nation, and I will bless you and make your name great; and so, you shall be a blessing; I will bless those who bless you and the one who curses you I will curse. And in you, all the <u>families of the earth shall be blessed</u>" (Genesis 12:1-3).

In Genesis 12:7, the Lord appeared to Abram and said, "To your descendants, I will give this land," and this became an inheritance to Abram. Romans 4:13 says, "For the promise to Abraham or to his descendants that Abraham would be heir of the world." Paul interprets the giving of land as a reference to the entire world. Prophetically, Israel's land is the whole world.

"I/God will make Abraham's <u>descendants as the dust</u>, the ground of the earth, so that if a man could number the dust of the earth, then your descendants also could be numbered" (Genesis 13:16). God promised to multiply Abraham's descendants greatly, and this will continue in the Millennium.

God promised to establish an eternal (forever) covenant not only with Abraham but also with his descendants in Genesis 17:7. "And I will establish My covenant between Me and you/Abraham and *your descendants after you*, throughout their generations for an everlasting covenant, to be God to you and to your descendants after you (Abraham). And I will give to you the land of your sojourning's, all the land of Canaan, for an everlasting possession, and I will be their (the descendants) God." This is a forever covenant with Abraham's descendants that has not been fulfilled. These descendants are precious to God. Zechariah 2:8 calls the descendants the apple of God's eye.

God's promise on the occasion of Abraham's sacrifice of his son Isaac, "Because you have done this thing and have not withheld your son, indeed I will greatly bless you, and I will greatly multiply your seed (Israel) as the stars of the heaven and as the sand which is on the seashore; and your seed, (your descendants) shall possess the gate (to own their enemies). In your seed Abraham, all the nations (Jews and Gentiles) of the earth shall be blessed because you obeyed My voice" (Genesis 22:16-18).

In Galatians 3:16, Paul tells us, "And to your Seed, that is *Christ*." Christ, who is the lineage of Abraham by this Seed, shows all people can have a relationship with God the Father. Christ's work makes it possible for God to be our God, according to the promise of Genesis 17:7-8. "I will establish My covenant between Me and you/Abraham and your descendants throughout their generations for an everlasting covenant, to be God to you and your descendants after you. And I will be their God." Christ is indeed a blessing to all nations and our way to be with the Father. God talks to Abraham's grandson Jacob and gives Jacob the new name, Israel, and Genesis 35:11-12 restates specific promises God had earlier made to Abraham. "I am God Almighty; be fruitful and multiply; a nation and a company of nations shall come from you, Abraham, and kings shall come forth from you, Jacob. And the land which I gave Abraham and Isaac, I give to you, Jacob, and I/God will give the land to your descendants after you/Jacob."

"By faith Abraham lived in the land of promise as a foreign land, dwelling in tents with son Isaac and grandson Jacob, fellow heirs of the same promise. For Abraham was looking for the city which has foundations, whose architect and builder is God" (Hebrews 11:9-10). This eternal scripture states that Abraham was looking for the New Heaven and the New Earth to come.

"And all these, (Abraham, Isaac, Jacob, the patriarchs) having gained approval through their faith but then, *did not* receive <u>what was promised them</u>, because God had provided something *better for us*" (Hebrews 11:39). That promise is Eternity, beyond the land that was promised to Abraham.

Not only did Israel receive *promises*, but the nation also received *blessings*.

"By faith, Isaac blessed his two sons, Jacob and Esau, concerning things to come" (Hebrews 11:20). Isaac's blessing to Jacob is important for two reasons:

First, God renamed Jacob, giving him the new name Israel. The children of Israel were literally just that, the descendants of Jacob through his twelve sons. In renaming Jacob, God identified the principal tribes of Israel. The twelve sons of Israel in birth order are Reuben, Simeon, Levi, Judah, Dan, Naphtali, Gad, Asher, Issachar, Zebulun, Joseph, and Benjamin. Each was the father of a tribe. Jacob's blessing concerns "things to come." It is prophetic, looking forward to Israel's future.

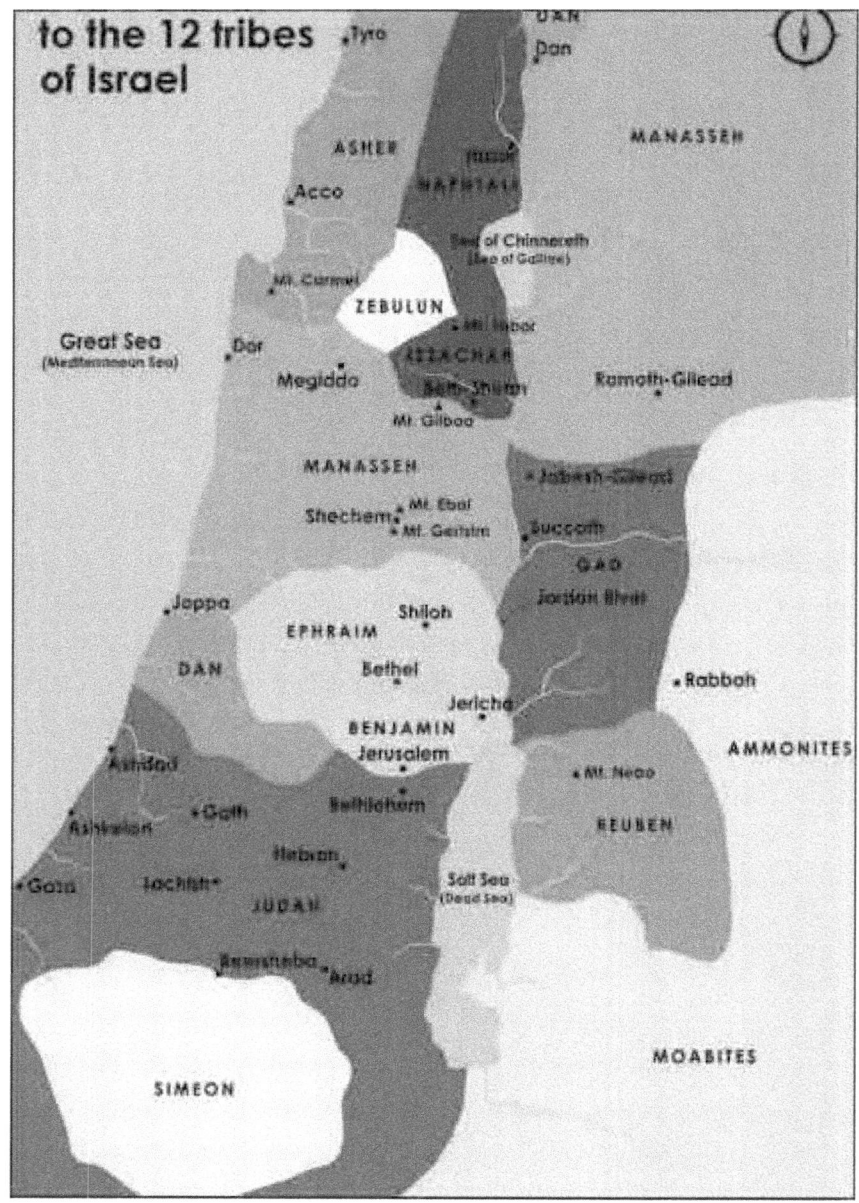

The map shows where the 12 tribes of Israel settled.

These are the promises God made to the patriarchs, Abraham, Isaac, and Jacob, as well as the blessings. The promises and blessings provide a good part of the information necessary to identify Israel throughout history. What makes the promises and the blessings so important today is the fact that they have not been prophetically finalized or fully fulfilled.

The Division of the Twelve Tribes of Israel

Abraham, Isaac, and Jacob were the start of the lineage of the twelve tribes of Israel. God changed Jacob's name to Israel because Jacob was *willing to let God govern his life*. Israel means "let God prevail." God then promised Jacob/Israel that all the blessings He/God had pronounced upon Jacob's grandfather Abraham would also be Jacob's/Israel's.

The name Israel often refers to all the descendants of Jacob as "the children of Israel," a term used in the first five books of the Bible for all twelve tribes. Literally speaking, it refers to all the descendants of the man Jacob/Israel.

A shortage of food later forced the Israelites to leave Canaan, and many moved to Egypt, where the leader, Pharaoh, enslaved them. After many generations, the Israelites left Egypt during the Exodus. God promised to guide the Israelites with Moses safely back to Canaan. They spent forty years wandering in the desert with Moses outside of the promised land. Once in the land of Canaan, the promised land, each of the twelve Israelite tribes settled in a different region or territory on either side of the Jordan River. Each was the father of a tribe of Israel.

As soon as the twelve tribes of Israel entered the promised land, the promised land started to prosper. They were blessed, but over time they became complacent. The people of Israel started looking around at all the countries surrounding them, and they said, "They all have kings. Why do we have to be the one nation with an invisible King?" (1 Samuel 8:1-10). So, Israel went to its spiritual leader, the prophet Samuel and said, "Samuel, give us a human king. We know God is King, but we want to be like all the other nations." Samuel was grieved. Samuel went to the Lord saying, "They want a human King. What should we do?" God responds, "Listen to the voice of the people, and all they say to you, for they have not rejected you, Samuel. Today, they have rejected me from being king over them" (1 Samuel 8:7).

The first of the kings was King Saul, his daughter married David. After King David's death, his son King Solomon ruled the <u>twelve tribes</u> of the united kingdom of Israel for forty years.

King Solomon died around 930 B.C. after building the beautiful temple in Jerusalem to house the Ark of the Covenant, which held the tablets inscribed with the Ten Commandments. After the death of King Solomon, his son King Rehoboam tried to increase his dictatorial rule with huge taxes and levies over the twelve tribes.

The ten northern tribes rebelled against King Rehoboam's harsh rule and gave their allegiance to a man named Jeroboam, making him their king. The ten northern tribes kept the name Israel.

The tribes of Judah and Benjamin did not agree with the proposed King of Israel, Rehoboam. They decided to forsake their inheritance and became the southern Kingdom of Judah.

The powerful tribe of Ephraim led the ten northern tribes in a successful revolt against the two southern tribes. This revolt established the ten northern tribes, the independent *Kingdom of Israel*, and Samaria became their capital. They were the tribes of Asher, Dan, Ephraim, Gad, Issachar, Manasseh, Naphtali, Reuben, Simeon, and Zebulun.

The two southern tribes Judah, and Benjamin, set up the *Kingdom of Judah*, and Jerusalem was their capital.

The ten tribes of Israel and the two tribes of Judah co-existed, although they often fought with each other. There were continuous wars, raids, and political maneuvering between the two rival kingdoms. As a result, the leadership of the ten tribes of Israel established an alternative temple in the capital of Samaria to encourage their people to ignore God's command to worship in Jerusalem during the three great annual festivals.

The northern kingdom set up golden calves in Dan and Bethel to prevent their people in the ten northern tribes from traveling south to Judah to worship in the true Temple in Jerusalem.

The Scripture declares in 1 Kings 12:19, "So Israel (the ten tribes) has been in rebellion against the house of David to this day." The two southern tribes, Judah and Benjamin stayed close to Jerusalem and remained loyal to King Solomon's descendants. Judah and Benjamin retained Jerusalem as the capital of their reduced kingdom.

After centuries of pagan worship, violence, and open idolatry, God sent the powerful Assyrian army to attack the unrepentant nation of northern Israel. The tribes of Israel east of the Jordan River were taken captive by Assyria. The ancient traditions of the Jews declare that the king of Assyria first invaded Israel in 747 B.C. and captured the golden calf at Dan. The Assyrians then led the tribes away into exile. Exile means the state of being barred or a period of forced absence from one's native country or home.

Twenty years later, in the second invasion, the armies of Assyria took Israel's capital, Samaria, and captured the entire nation of northern Israel, as recorded in II Kings 17:6. They carried off the second golden calf at Bethel together with the tribes leaving but one-eighth of the Israelites in their own land. This took ninety percent of Israel's population back to northern Assyria as captives.

The Assyrians did not leave the land deserted. They replaced the population of the land of Israel with other captives from the Assyrian empire. The King of Assyria brought people from five different regions and settled them in the towns the Israelites once occupied. This was intended to make sure the Israelite captives would not have any motivation to rebel against the Assyrian Empire and go back to Israel. The ten northern tribes were forced to intermarry with the Assyrian people so they would stay in Assyria.

The captives of the ten tribes were exiled and settled in the area the ancient Greeks called *Adiabene*. They were also settled in the areas to the north of ancient Nineveh and Babylon. This is in present-day northern Iraq, Iran, and Afghanistan. Gradually over the years, these Israelites settled as colonists throughout north Mesopotamia. By 536 B.C., the northern Israelites had been settlers for one hundred and eighty- five years. Gradually over the years, these Israelites settled as colonists throughout northern Mesopotamia. Their close ties to the Holy Land had been broken.

Of the millions from the ten tribes of Israel taken captive, it is estimated that less than one percent of these captives from Israel ever returned. The vast majority of the Israelites from the ten tribes remained in these locations and were lost to history. They became known as the ten lost tribes of Israel.

The Two Southern Tribes of Judah

In 606 B.C., the Babylonian King Nebuchadnezzar and his armies invaded the Southern Kingdom of Judah and conquered the city of Jerusalem. During three series of conquests, King Nebuchadnezzar took vast numbers of captives from the land of Judah back to Babylon, including the prophets Daniel and Ezekiel. After a brutal siege, the armies of Babylon destroyed the city of Jerusalem and the beautiful Temple.

The seventy-year captivity in Babylon ended as prophesied in Jeremiah 25:11. "And this whole land (Judah) shall be a desolation and a horror, and these nations shall serve the King of Babylon seventy years." After seventy years, a decree allowed the Jews to return in freedom to their homeland. However, only forty-two thousand of the Jews in Babylon chose to return to Jerusalem and Judah, which is less than five percent. The great majority of the forty-two thousand Jews returning were from the tribes of Judah and Benjamin, with a small scattering of Levites.

Those who returned from Babylon rebuilt their country over a period of five centuries until their people fell again into terrible apostasy. Apostasy is the abandonment of a religious belief and rejection of God's laws. The Roman armies attacked and destroyed Jerusalem and the Temple in 70 A.D. Once again, the people from the land of Judah were dispersed as exiles among the nations.

An important message to mention here is about the word "Jew." The term "Jew" is a shortened word for Judah. After being taken captive by Babylon, the people of Judah became known as the "Jews." The King James Version of the Bible called the men of Judah the "Jews." After many centuries of exile, all exiled tribes are commonly referred to as "Jews."

The ultimate restoration and reconciliation of the ten tribes of Israel and the two tribes of Judah were prophesied by the prophet Ezekiel while he was in captivity in Babylon.

Ezekiel 37:21-22 states the Lord God said, "Behold/Surely I will take the sons/children of Israel from among the nations wherever they have gone, and I will gather them from every side and bring them into their own land; and I will make them one nation in the land, on the mountains of Israel; and one king shall be king over them; they will no longer be two nations; they will no longer be divided into two kingdoms."

In this prophecy, God states that He will restore the ten lost tribes of Israel in the last days and unite them with the two tribes of Judah forever. For twenty-five hundred years, this prophecy has remained unfulfilled.

The prophet Ezekiel declares that God will *allocate the land of Israel* between the *twelve tribes* after the Messiah appears at His Second Coming. Ezekiel provides a very detailed description of the allotment of the land for the descendant of Israel that will take place in the Millennium (Ezekiel 47:13-29).

During the time of exile, all twelve tribes became slaves to the Gentile people. This was from the consequences of the Israelite people for their rejection of God's law. God dispersed the Israelites using the Assyrians and Babylonians.

God tells us none will be lost in Amos 9:9. "I will shake the house of Israel among all nations as grain is shaken in a sieve, but not a kernel will fall to the ground." This scripture states that God separated His people and scattered them while at the same time keeping track of every one of them. God's Word states where to look for Israel. Psalms say they are scattered somewhere over oceans and rivers. Isaiah 11:11 says they are "Scattered over the islands of the sea." Jeremiah 3:12-13 says, "Go and proclaim these words toward the *north* and say return faithless Israel."

In Jeremiah 31:10, God says, "O Nations and coastlands far off who scattered Israel will also gather them as a shepherd does his flock." These are islands far away from the northwest of Jerusalem. God's Word speaks from the Book of Jeremiah and tells us from where He will gather Israel in the last days, from the *north,* the *coastlands,* and *islands* far away.

Jeremiah 23 explains that the days are coming when God will destroy those who scattered His people. The ones that scattered God's people did not take care of them, and God will attend to them for the evil of their deeds against His Jewish people. During the Tribulation, God will deal with the ones that scattered His people.

God will gather the remnant of His people from these countries at the end of the Tribulation and bring them back to their homeland in Israel. They will be fruitful and multiply during the Millennium. God says He shall raise up shepherds to be over them (that will be the Saints who will rule and reign with Jesus), and they (the Saints) will take care of His people (the Jews), and none will be missing. God knows where all the descendants of His people are. Jeremiah is saying God will gather His people, the remnant in the latter day, out of the countries and bring them back to Israel, their homeland in the Millennium.

In Jeremiah 31:8-9, God says He will bring the remnant of Israel from the northern country and gather them from the remote parts of the earth from around the world. With weeping, they shall come, and with their repentance, He will lead them. Weeping means the Israelite remnant, the descendants, will realize who Jesus is and that their ancestors had persecuted Him. They will come with weeping and much repentance.

Although God has made it clear who makes up the descendants of Israel today, many Jewish people do not know about their true identity. They dwell in the darkness of their heritage because their forefathers rejected God long ago.

Isaiah 11:11-12, and God says, "Then it will happen on the *day of the Lord* (the Second Coming of Jesus). He will again gather His people the second time with His hand, the remnant of His people who remain from Assyria and other countries and from the island of the sea. He will lift up standards for the nations (in the Millennium), and will assemble the banished ones of Israel (the ten tribes), and will gather the dispersed of Judah (the two tribes) from the four corners of the earth." This indicates that the descendants will have migrated far and wide. God will gather them and call them to greater things in the Millennium.

The scriptures say all of Israel will be saved. Acts 2:16-21 is spoken through the prophet Joel, and He talks about the last days when God will pour out His spirit upon all mankind, and it shall be that <u>everyone who calls</u> on the name of the Lord shall be saved.

This is still going on today and has yet to be fulfilled. The mystery is that God has partially hardened the hearts of the Jewish people. They cannot hear all of the Gospel or the salvation message until God is ready. This is so the Gentile, the non-Jewish people, the church is saved, or as the scripture states, the fullness of the Gentile has happened.

To summarize these scriptures would be to say that Abraham and his seed were promised the land as an inheritance. Later generations had hardened hearts and followed idols. God used Assyria and the Babylonians to scatter His people from their land. God sent Jesus, and the Gentiles were grafted in. We will see how God will get His people's attention by sending judgments to the earth in the Tribulation. We will eventually see Israel regathered as Jesus makes His Second Coming. His people will be restored and enter the Millennium, where they will be cared for. They will get their promised land back in Israel in the Millennial Kingdom.

Chapter Eight

◇◇◇◇

UNDERSTANDING THE BOOK OF REVELATION

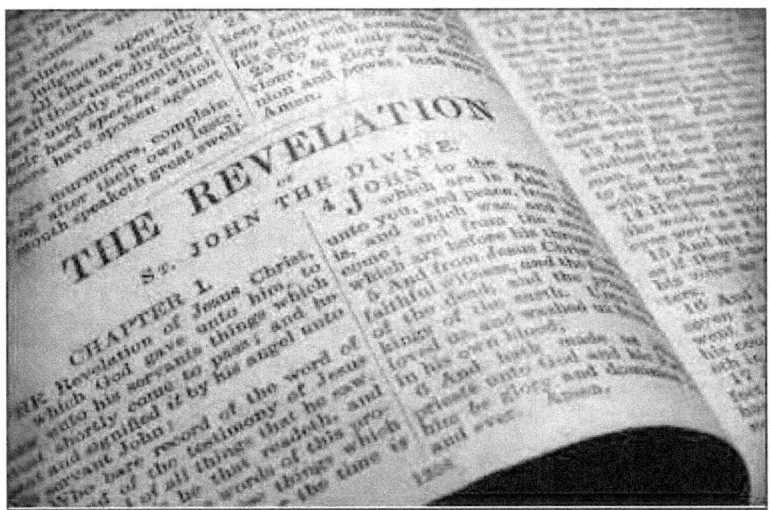

I FIND THE Book of Revelation very interesting and intriguing, and there is so much information for us to learn. I taught the subjects in the Book of Revelation for several years. It is packed full of information we need to understand about prophecy and the end times and what will occur on earth while we are in Heaven. There is more written about what the unbeliever will experience in the Tribulation than there is about what believers experience in Heaven.

Apostle John wrote the Book of Revelation in the genre of apocalyptic literature. This was recognized as an acceptable form of writing literature in Biblical times. In Jesus' time, people understood that writers of apocalyptic literature claimed to have had a supernatural and prophetic revelation from God. In this style of literature, the writer uses symbols, visions, metaphors, and language to communicate heavenly realities. Apocalyptic literature was not always taken literally but understood as prophetic and spiritual truth. The last part of the Book of Daniel is an excellent example of apocalyptic literature as Daniel gives prophesy of the future.

Apocalyptic literature is not a common form of literature for modern readers. Apostle John, the revealer of the Book of Revelation, wrote and saw into the spiritual realm, which he reveals through symbolism and metaphors. The first-century believers would have clearly understood John's message in the Book of Revelation. We must understand John's writings in the context of the time he was living in. We cannot take what John saw and spoke and try to make it fit into our modern times and terms. I always teach that we must think back to Apostle John's time to understand what John was thinking and talking about in the Book of Revelation.

The key to understanding the Book of Revelation is discerning and deciding what is literal, a metaphor, and what is symbolic. Literal is taking the words as they are written. A metaphor is a figure of speech that states that one thing is another thing. It is used to make comparisons between two objects. Symbolism serves as a representation carrying an even greater meaning of what it represents. An example of symbolism is a smile as a gesture of welcome or a wedding ring as a representation of marriage.

The Book of Revelation is about the Tribulation and the events leading up to and climaxing with the Second Coming of Christ. It also encompasses the Millennial Kingdom teaching and the eternal life that will follow. It is the only book in the Bible that promises a special *blessing* in studying the book. In Revelation 1:3, Jesus tells us, "*Blessed* is he who *reads* and those who *hear* the words of the prophecy and *heed* the things which are written in it: for the time is near." We are <u>promised</u> that we will be blessed by reading, hearing, and studying the Book of Revelation and paying attention to the words of prophecy.

Revelation 1:1 states that God gave the uncovering and the unveiling of Jesus Christ to Jesus, then Jesus gave that message to His angel. Jesus' angel gave the message to John, and John gives the message to the believers. John is the revealer of the Book of Revelation to us.

The story is revealed in the first half and then explained in the second half of the Book of Revelation. That is why we think we have already read something or are reading the book over again. It is revealing and then explaining. We also need to understand that the Book of Revelation is not in chronological order. There are interludes between events.

An interlude is parenthetical information that interrupts the chronological order or flow to give the reader valuable information. It is the type of information that would leave you in the dark if you were not given it. It is the information we need to know in order to understand better what is taking place. You will find I will use interludes in writing this book. You might think something is out of order, but I will use an interlude, so you will understand better what is to follow or is happening. This is like an FYI or for your information.

The Book of Revelation has an outline. In Revelation 1:19, the outline is told to John and for John to write.

1. Write the things you, *John, have seen,* this is the visions of Jesus in chapter 1.

2. And the things *which are,* these are the things concerning the churches of Apostle John's time, which John writes in chapters 2 and 3.

3. And the things *which shall take place* after the churches in Chapters 4-22.

This is the three-fold division of the Book of Revelation. John writes the things he *saw* and the things which *are.* Then John is told to come up into Heaven to be shown the things which *must happen.* Revelation 4:1 states specifically, "after these things." I believe this means <u>after</u> the events of Revelation in the Tribulation chapters 4-22 must occur after the church, when the believers are taken to Heaven.

The Twenty-Four Elders and The Four Living Ones

Let us read what John sees in Heaven around the throne of God. In Revelation 4:6-10, John sees twenty-four elders and the four living beasts or creatures around the throne of God. That informs us that these two groups are very important, and we need to understand who they are.

In Revelation 4:4, John sees twenty-four thrones around God's throne, and sitting on the thrones are twenty-four Elders clothed in white garments and golden crowns on their heads. Twenty-four in the Old Testament is associated with the priesthood. An Elder in the Bible is a leader or ruler who is valued for wisdom and holds a position of responsibility and authority.

The priesthood of Israel was a male individual who, according to the Hebrew Bible, were descendants of Aaron and the tribe of Levi. They served in the Tabernacle and in the Temple. In King David's time, there were thousands of priests, so King David divided them into twenty-four groups, and the twenty-four represented all the priests. The twenty- four Elders John sees before the throne could easily be representing all the Saints.

The Elders around the throne are wearing white raiment. A raiment is usually made of linen cloth and represents justification meaning free from all things. White raiment is used in the Book of Revelation of Christ and of the Saints. Revelation 3:5 says he who overcomes shall be clothed in white garments. In 6:11, a white robe was given to each of the Tribulation Saints. In Revelation 19:8, the Bride of Christ is clothed in fine linen, bright and pure, for the fine linen is the righteous deeds and acts of the Saints.

The Elders are also wearing golden crowns, this is the victory crown meaning they are saved and have overcome the world. The Elders are very important and are in several scriptures talking to John in Heaven. In Revelation 5-5, one of the Elders said to John to stop weeping. In 7:13, one of the Elders tells John who the multitude is under the altar.

Who are these Elders? The Bible does not directly tell us who they are. What we do know is that the twenty-four Elders are righteous Saints clothed in linen and wearing victory crowns. I believe the Elders are the twelve tribes of Israel and the twelve apostles and are representing the Old and New Testament Saints.

Let us learn about the four living ones that are also around the throne. The King James Bible refers to the four as the four beasts, and the New

American Standard calls them the four living creatures. I believe they are referred to as beasts and creatures because of the way the Bible describes the way they look.

I like to refer to them as the four living ones. They are not what we think of as beasts or creatures, but they are living beings in Heaven. Revelation 4:6 states that around the throne are the four living ones, full of eyes in front and behind. This means they see everything. Revelation 4:7-8 states, "And the first creature was like a lion, and the second creature like an ox, and the third creature had a face like that of a man, and the fourth creature was like a flying eagle. And the four living creatures, each one of them having six wings, are full of eyes around and within; and day and night they do not cease to say, Holy, Holy, Holy is the Lord God, the Almighty, who was and who is and who is to come." You are favored by God because Jesus "is." You are forgiven by God because Jesus "was." You are not forsaken by God because Jesus "is to come."

What we know is that the living ones are on the four sides of the throne, never ceasing to praise God. They have a face with a lion, a calf/ox, a face of a man, and an eagle. These four faces represent the strong lion the king of the wild beast, the ox for the domestic animal, the face of a man for the earth, and the eagle for the king of the air.

The four living ones could be a combination between the Seraphim and the Cherubim angels, as described in Isiah and Ezekiel.

Isiah 6:1-3 describes Seraphim angels as six-winged beings that fly around the Throne of God crying Holy, Holy, Holy. The guardians of God's throne giving their praises to God.

Ezekiel 1:5-21 and 10:20-21 gives a very detailed description of the Cherubim, explaining the four faces and the eyes. The wings are to move where ever they want. With their faces, they can move in any direction without ever turning their head. Their eyes see everything, nothing is hidden. Ezekiel calls them living beings.

The Seven Years of the Tribulation

I believe the born-again Christian believer in Jesus Christ will be in Heaven during the seven years of the Tribulation. There are no instructions in the New Testament telling the believers how to live during the Tribulation.

The apparent reason is that the believers in Christ will not be living on earth because they will be in Heaven. The Church, the Body of Christ, is mentioned in the Book of Revelation in chapters one through three and not again until chapter nineteen. Further, the Church is not mentioned in Revelation six through eighteen, known as the Tribulation chapters.

While the believers are in Heaven, the seven years of the Tribulation will take place on this earth. 1 Thessalonians 5:9 states, "For God has not destined us for wrath." We, the believer, will not enter or go through the wrath of the Tribulation.

After the Rapture of the believers to Heaven, the <u>unbelievers</u> all over the world will stay on this earth to endure the time in the Tribulation. They will most likely continue to live in the same city, in the same house, drive the same cars, and go to the same stores. Their life surroundings will be the same when the Tribulation begins, except for the chaos and confusion the believers make when they leave this earth in the Rapture. The definition of Tribulation means the state of great trouble and suffering. God will finish His discipline of Israel and finalize His judgment of the unbelieving world in the Tribulation.

One of the purposes of the Tribulation in relation to Israel is the conversion of the Jewish remnant and faith in Jesus as their Messiah. This will take place throughout the Tribulation. By the end of the seven- year period, the number that will convert to Jesus is likely to be a third of the Jewish people. Zechariah 13:9 states, "And I will bring the third part through the fire, refine them as silver is refined, and test them as gold is tested. They will call on My name, and I will answer them. God will say, "They are My people," and they will say, "The Lord is my God."

As part of the process of bringing the Jewish remnant to faith, Zechariah 13:8 speaks of the purging of the unbelieving Jewish people from the nation. "And it will come about in all the land that two parts in it will be cut off and perish, but the third will be left in it." The Old Testament prophets speak often of the purging out of the Jewish people. Throughout Scripture, the Tribulation is also referred to by other names. In Isaiah 2:12, Isaiah 13:6-9, and 1 Thessalonians 5:2, the Tribulation is called "the Day of the Lord." Daniel 12:1 calls it "the time or day of trouble." Jeremiah 30:7 calls the Tribulation "the time of Jacob's trouble." Matthew 24:21

calls it "the great tribulation," which refers to the more intense second half of the seven years.

Jesus tells His disciples in Matthew 24:21, "For then there will be great tribulation, such that has not occurred since the beginning of the world until now, nor ever shall." This tribulation will be greater than any of the wars this earth has ever known. Greater than WWI and greater than the holocaust of WWII.

The first half of the Tribulation will bring one of the biggest revivals this world has ever known. A great harvest of souls for Christ will take place. The Gospel of the Kingdom is preached by the 144,000 Jewish Witnesses in the Tribulation. The people will hear that Jesus' Kingdom is coming. "And this gospel of the (Millennial) kingdom shall be preached in the whole world for a witness to all the nations, and then the end shall come (Second Coming)" (Matthew 24:14). The people who accept this message of the Kingdom of Jesus will be part of the great redeemed multitude saved during the Tribulation.

The people in the Tribulation who begin to understand what is happening, see and hear the truth, believe in the Gospel, and understand that Jesus' Millennial Kingdom is coming. They will call on others to repent and believe, and they will endure great persecution. The Antichrist and his followers will not tolerate their evangelism and will likely kill them. Many who thought they were saved and were left behind will be searching. Revelation 7:4-8 tells us that many will hear the Gospel from the 144,000 Jewish Witnesses. We could also call the 144,000 missionaries because they will reach multitudes from every corner of the world.

Revelation 11:3-12 tells us there will also be Two Prophets who will prophesy in Jerusalem for 1,260 days, the first three and a half years of the Tribulation. They will perform great miracles and preach in the Temple to the priest about Jesus.

Revelation 14:12-13 states the perseverance and the endurance of the Saints who keep and obey the general rules of God, and their faith in Jesus during the Tribulation will be *blessed*. Why blessed in such a horrible time? Because as believers, even if they die, they will enter the Millennial Kingdom and Eternity. There are only three ways to get out of the Tribulation. One is to die, the second is to be killed, and the third is to live through the seven years of great persecution.

Many believers will die for their faith, but in their death, they will have eternal life. God will take care of them for their hardships in the Tribulation. Revelation 7:15–17 says God will spread his covering over them. Never again will they hunger or thirst. The sun and scorching will not beat upon them. For Jesus will be their shepherd and will lead them to the living water, and every tear will be wiped away. These scriptures tell us some of what the people who will die will have endured, and God will now take care of them forever.

Revelation 7:9 starts out with "After these things." When you see the phrase "after these things" in scripture, it is very important to look back in scripture to see "after *what* things." In Revelation 7:9, "After these things," is speaking about the 144,000 Jewish Witnesses.

After the 144,000 witnessing in the Tribulation, this is what John sees in Heaven. "After these things (the 144,000 witnessing) I, John, looked and behold a great multitude which no one could count, from every nation, and all tribes and people and tongues (languages) <u>standing before the throne</u> and before the Lamb, clothed in white robe, (salvation) and palm branches (victory) in their hands; and they cried out with a loud voice, saying, Salvation to our God who sits on the throne, and to the Lamb" (Revelation 7:9-11). These in Heaven that died in the Tribulation are called the Tribulation Saints.

When John asks who they are, he is told by an Elder. "These are the ones who have come out of the great tribulation; they have washed their robes and made them white in the blood of Jesus" (Revelation 7:14). The Tribulation Saints are set apart as wearing white robes. The meaning of washing their robes and making them white (pure) in the blood of Jesus is that they have received salvation.

Some might ask, why not live as we want now on this earth? We will have another chance to be saved in the Tribulation. This is true, there will be another chance to be saved in the Tribulation. That is because God is a loving God that gives unbelievers chance after chance to be saved, including in the Tribulation. But, let us take a further look into what will take place in the Tribulation and see if you would really want to wait and be in the Tribulation.

All the believers will have been taken out in the Rapture, leaving only unbelievers to live on earth. The persecution is what should give anyone hesitation with the thought of waiting. Many criminals, rapists, and other violent and harsh people will be left on the earth to live with. The living conditions will be frightening and chaotic, and there will be no moral code. The conditions of the concentration war camp should come to mind when thinking of the Tribulation.

The Tribulation *will not* be peaceful, and the people will go through persecution, scary times, and famines. They will watch their loved ones killed, have their homes vandalized, and even have their homes taken from them, resulting in being homeless. Food will be in short supply, and everything they have ever known could be destroyed before they are saved.

Those that wait and are the newly saved believers in the Tribulation will experience a considerable amount of persecution. Then possibly experience a horrifying death, being killed or dying as a martyr. Remember, they must experience death in the Tribulation before they would go to Heaven.

The Tribulation will be a time of great trouble for the saved and the unsaved people because of both the unbeliever's persecution and God's judgments that He will pour out on the earth. Over half of the population of the world will have been killed by the middle of the Tribulation.

As God is dealing out His just punishment on an unbelieving world, God will restore Israel to faith and extend grace to all who believe, both the Jews and the Gentiles. God will have two special groups to witness to the unbelievers during the Tribulation. They will reach many with the message of salvation. They are the 144,000 Jewish Witnesses and the Two Prophets.

Next, we will learn about some of the key subjects of the Tribulation. They are the 144,000 Jewish Witnesses, the Two Prophets, the Antichrist, the False Prophet, and the Mark of the Beast.

The 144,000 Jewish Witnesses

The 144,000 Jewish Witnesses enter the Tribulation as unbelievers. We know this because all the believers will have been taken in the Rapture, and only unbelievers will be left. The 144,000 chosen Jewish Witnesses will receive their salvation at the beginning of the Tribulation, and God will set them apart (sanctified) for His purpose.

Revelation 7:4-8 explains that these chosen 144,000 Jewish bondservants (followers of Christ) will be descendants of the twelve tribes of Israel. There will be 12,000 Jewish bondservants, followers from each of the twelve tribes totaling 144,000. Revelation 7:3 states they will have a seal of protection on their forehead given to them by God. They will be supernaturally protected from the persecution of the unbelieving people and from the seal and trumpet judgments of God that will take place during the first three and a half years of their witnessing.

The purpose of the 144,000 Jewish Witnesses is to communicate to the unsaved people the salvation message, the Gospel of Jesus Christ, and the coming of Jesus' Millennial Kingdom. They will witness all over the world. The 144,000 Jewish Witnesses are introduced in Revelation 7:4-8.

We do not hear about them again until Revelation 14:1-5 when they are finished with their witnessing and are in Heaven. "John looked and behold the Lamb/Jesus was standing on Mount Zion and with Him are one hundred and forty-four thousand, having His name (Jesus) and the name of His Father (God) written on their foreheads."

They are not on Mount Zion in Jerusalem on earth, they are on heavenly Mount Zion. Hebrews 12:2 tells us, "But you have come to Mount Zion and to the city of the living God, the heavenly Jerusalem and to myriads of angels, to the general assembly (meeting) and church of the first-born (priority) who are enrolled in the heavens and to God." Revelation 14:3 states that the 144,000 are in Heaven before the throne. "And they sang a new song before the throne and before the four living ones and the elders, and no one could learn the song except the one hundred and forty-four thousand who had been purchased (salvation) from the earth." This scripture tells us they are before the throne in Heaven. In Revelation 14:4-5, the scripture gives us a good description of the 144,000. "These are the ones who have not been defiled by women (idols), for they have kept themselves chaste (pure). These are the ones who follow the Lamb (Jesus) wherever He goes. These have been purchased (salvation, redeemed) from among men as first fruits (dedicated) to God and to the Lamb. And no lie (deception) was found in their mouth; they are blameless (without blemish)." They are before the throne of God.

The Two Prophets

The Two Prophets, which God refers to as My Two Witnesses is showing a special relationship with God that was not shared with other witnesses in the Bible (Revelation 11:3). God will grant authority and power to His Two Prophets, who will prophesy for the first three and a half years, or 1,260 days of the Tribulation. These two will be true prophets, speaking by divine revelation and performing miracles under the authority of God. They will be clothed in sackcloth as if in mourning. The first half of the Tribulation will be one of the greatest spiritual awakenings in the history of mankind as the Two Prophets are in Jerusalem and in the Temple prophesying, and the 144,000 Jewish witnesses will be all over the world witnessing.

The Two Prophets play a major role in Israel being converted. One of the prophets will be Elijah from the Old Testament. This is prophesied in Malachi 4:5-6 saying Elijah will return in the last days. This is the last prophecy in the Old Testament. It concerns the return of Elijah, the prophet, to the earth from Heaven shortly before Jesus's Second Coming. Malachi 4:5 reads, "Behold, I am going to send you Elijah the prophet before the coming of the great and terrible day of the Lord." The great and terrible day of the Lord (Second Coming of Jesus) means it will be great for the righteous but dreadful and terrible for the wicked.

We do not know for sure the identity of the second witness. Some speculate it will be Moses, and some say, Enoch. There are scriptures supporting both.

The Two Prophets will be in the Temple and will prophesy to the Jewish Priest and the Jewish people. They will reveal the spiritual significance of everything the priest does and how it points to Jesus as the Messiah. They will also be prophesying to the people around the temple that have come to make their sacrifices. They will prophesy that Jesus is the Messiah and that He has already sacrificed once for us all. The Two Prophets will make many angry with their prophecies.

Revelation 11:6 says that if any man desires to harm them, fire (the Word of God) will proceed out of the mouths of the Two Witnesses, and they can devour (kill) their enemies, the unbelievers. If the unbelievers provoke the Two Witnesses, they have the power and authority to shut up the sky so rain will not fall on their enemy's land. They can turn the waters into blood and smite the earth with every plague as often as they desire. They will have power from God.

In the middle of the Tribulation, "When the Two Prophets have finished their testimony, the beast that comes up out of the abyss, will make war with them, and overcome them and kill them" (Revelation 11:7). Coming up out of the abyss tells us this is the demonic spirit of Satan and will dwell in the man known as the Antichrist. The Antichrist will kill the Two Prophets by the power and authority of Satan.

The Two Witnesses' dead bodies will lie in the street of Jerusalem for three and a half days. The unbelievers will not permit the Two Witnesses' dead bodies to be buried or laid in a tomb. This will be a great dishonor to the Two Witnesses because it is a great indignation not to bury or lay their bodies in a tomb immediately.

Revelation 11:8 (KJV) tells us, "And their dead bodies shall lie in the street of the great city which spiritually is called Sodom and Egypt, where also their Lord was crucified."

This scripture tells us several things. The great city where the Two Prophets' will die is Jerusalem because that is where the Lord was crucified. Spiritually Jerusalem is being called Sodom and Egypt. Sodom refers to sexual immorality, and Egypt refers to the slavery of God's people. This is telling us that at the time of the Two Prophets' death, the city of Jerusalem in the Tribulation will be so corrupt that the Bible calls Jerusalem the same as Sodom.

The unbelieving people will rejoice and celebrate this great occasion because of the torment the Two Prophets inflicted on them. The people will even send gifts to one another. They will be very happy that the Two Witnesses have been killed (Revelation 11:10).

After three and a half days of lying dead in the street, the *breath of life* from God, the spirit of God, will enter the Two Witnesses. They will stand up on their feet, and great fear and terror will fall upon those watching (Revelation 11:11).

The Two Witnesses will hear a loud voice from Heaven saying to them to come up to Heaven. "And they will go up into Heaven in the cloud, and their enemies will watch them go in disbelief" (Revelation 11:12). The Jews will see this as similar to Jesus' death on the cross and His resurrection when Jesus went up in the clouds to Heaven.

Revelation 11:13 tells us, "At the same hour, there was a great earthquake, and a tenth of Jerusalem fell, and seven thousand people were killed in the earthquake and the rest will be terrified and will give glory to God in heaven." The majority of the people who are in Jerusalem are Jews, and they will give their Glory or full recognition and repentance to God. The eyes of the Jewish people are opened for the first time. They realize they missed that Jesus was the Messiah, and they will give Glory to God. Glory in the Bible here, depicts repentance. They will repent and give glory as they finally realize that Jesus is the Messiah. The Antichrist is not going to have this, and the Jews must flee for their life.

The man called the Antichrist could not enter the Temple in the first half of the Tribulation because of the Jewish people and the Two Prophets. Now that the power to destroy is gone that the Two Prophets had, and the Jewish people believe in Jesus. The Antichrist will break his contract with Israel and then will destroy the Temple. This is what causes the Abomination that causes the Desolation of the Temple at the mid-point of the Tribulation.

The Antichrist

The definition of the Antichrist is a person, a force against or opposing Christ. We get so captivated by the word Antichrist that we forget the Antichrist will be a human person. He will be an unbeliever living on this earth when the Rapture takes place, and he will be left behind. This person will enter the Tribulation as an unbeliever.

This person will be a very intelligent, and deceptive person who wants power and to take over the world. He will be a political, commercial, military, and religious genius. He will be an excellent speaker, and the people will believe in and follow him. He will be in leadership, and he will be working on his evil intentions throughout the first half of the Tribulation.

The first part of the Tribulation is political. This person will make an agreement, a covenant with Israel to bring peace, and the solutions to political problems that Israel will desperately need. At the time of the signing of the agreement, the covenant, the people will not recognize this person as the Antichrist. He will be bringing peace to the people and solving an economic crisis.

In the middle of the Tribulation, after killing the Two Prophets, the Antichrist will break the covenant of peace with Israel, and put a stop to the daily sacrifice and offerings in the temple. He will destroy the temple in Jerusalem, and bring in the *Abomination of Desolation*. This is when the people will know he is the Antichrist, at the mid-point of the Tribulation. He will destroy the Temple and set up an image of himself in the temple, for the people to worship him. This image will move, speak and be able to communicate with the people.

According to Revelation 13:4, the Antichrist will be given all of Satan's power and authority during the Tribulation. In Revelation 13:1, the Antichrist is referred to as the Beast coming out of the sea. I believe from my studies that the word "sea" is a metaphor for evil and also a metaphor for a large group of people, a sea of people. The Beast, the Antichrist, will be coming out of a sea of evil people to take control, and not out of the sea of water.

Daniel 9:27 tells us about the Antichrist. "And he (the Antichrist) will make a firm covenant with many for one week (7 years), but in the middle of the week (3 and ½ years), he (the Antichrist) will put a stop to sacrifice and grain offering; and on the wing of abominations will come one (Antichrist) who makes desolate (destroy), even until a complete destruction." Daniel's prophecy from the Old Testament tells us this will happen. This prophecy has not yet been fulfilled.

The False Prophet

Another person, the False Prophet, will be introduced in the second half of the Tribulation to assist and further help the Antichrist. This man will have already been at work during the first half of the Tribulation but will not come into his full recognition as the False Prophet until the Antichrist comes into power.

The False Prophet can do all the same things the Antichrist can do when the False Prophet *is in the presence* of the Antichrist. Revelation 13:13 says the False Prophet will deceive the people by doing great miracles, and he will be able to make fire come down from Heaven on earth for the people to see.

The second half of the Tribulation will be about religion, and the False Prophet is the new religious leader. His purpose is to lead the people to worship the man and his image, the Antichrist.

The temple where the daily Jewish sacrifices will be held will be destroyed. This is known as the Abomination of Desolation (Daniel 9:27).

Abomination is described as idolatrous worship, indecency, and something disgusting or vile and detestable to God and His people.

Desolation is to destroy, devastate, desecrate, or violate something sacred and leave it in a horrible condition. The Abomination of Desolation of the Holy Temple will be despicable, disgusting, destroying, and violating to the sacred temple.

An image of the Antichrist will be erected in the temple by the False Prophet. Revelation 13:15 informs us that the False Prophet is given the power from Satan to give breath and life to the image so the image can speak. This image of the Antichrist will speak, move, communicate, and converse with the people. The False Prophet will demand the people to worship the image. Revelation 20:4 tells us that if the people do not worship the Antichrist's image, they will be beheaded.

Satan will give these two men, the Antichrist, and the False Prophet, complete power and authority to do Satan's work. The False Prophet will deceive the people and lead them to worship the man, the Antichrist. The False Prophet will establish false doctrines to help the Antichrist's political and religious power over the people. Their anti-god religion will be a faith system that Satan will use to unite the people in the Tribulation under the leadership of the Antichrist.

The Mark of the Beast

The believers will not take the mark of the beast because the believers will be in Heaven when this occurs on earth in the Tribulation.

When people hear the words Antichrist, Tribulation, or the Book of Revelation, they want to know about the mark of the beast and the number 666. The mark of the beast takes place in the latter part of the Tribulation. The mark of the Beast is the mark of the Antichrist. The Beast is another name given to the Antichrist and is explained in the Book of Revelation

13:16-18. The False Prophet will deceive and force all to get the mark of the Beast on their right hand or on their forehead. This mark will be a literal mark. People will need to have proof or evidence that they are a follower of the Antichrist to buy and sell to survive in the latter days of the Tribulation. The False Prophet requires that no one will be able to buy or sell except those who have the mark.

Revelation 13:17-18 states, that the mark is the name of the beast or the number of the Antichrist's name. The number of his name is that of a man, and his number is 666. There is so much more spiritually to the mark of the Beast than we will be able to cover here.

Revelation 19:20 tells us, "The beast (Antichrist) was seized, and with him, the false prophet who performed the signs in his (Antichrist) presence by which he (false prophet) deceived those who had received the mark of the beast and those who worshiped his image; these two were thrown alive into the lake of fire which burns with brimstone. And the rest (followers) were killed with the sword (Word of God) which came from the mouth of Him (Jesus) who sat upon the horse, and all the birds were filled with their flesh."

The story of Babylon is in Revelation Chapters 17 and 18. A whole book can be written about Babylon, and I am only going to touch on a few things here.

There are two different mentions of Babylon in the Book of Revelation. 1. The whore of Babylon, is the religious part of Babylon. 2. Babylon the Great is the city and empire.

Babylon is materialistic wealthy and a commercial empire.

1. She is a city.
2. She sits on seven hills which is Rome.
3. Her name is "Mystery Babylon," which is the code name for Rome.
4. She controls the life and lifestyles of people from almost every nation.
5. She is incredibly wealthy.

6. She became drunk on the blood of the people, meaning she kills many.

At the end of the Tribulation, the Book of Revelation refers to the city of Babylon. This city is Rome and is the Revived Roman Empire. The Antichrist and the False Prophet will use all their authority from Satan to empower and govern this corrupt government and commerce.

In the later part of the Tribulation, we know that most of the people will take the mark of the beast on their hand or forehead in order to buy and sell in Babylon. If they do not take the mark, they will be killed.

We learn in Revelation 16:12, in the Sixth Bowl of God's Wrath, that there are Kings and armies that are not under the Antichrist's rule. Not all people take the mark of the beast or follow the Antichrist. We will learn what happens to them later in the book under The Natural People of the Nations.

Next, we will learn about the Seven-Sealed Scroll, the Four Horsemen of the Apocalypse, the Seven Trumpet Judgments, and the Seven Bowls of Wrath.

The Seven-Sealed Scroll

Revelation chapters five, six, and eight starts by telling us what happens in the Tribulation with the opening of the Seven-Sealed Scroll. Revelation 5:1-5 says, "John saw in the right hand of God who sat on the throne a scroll written inside and on the back sealed up with seven seals." Typically, there was writing on only one side of a scroll. For a scroll to have writing on the inside and on the back means the scroll was very full.

In Revelation 5:2-4, "John saw an important angel proclaiming with a loud voice. Who is worthy to open the scroll and break its seals? No one in Heaven, or on the earth, or under the earth was able to open the scroll or look into it (inside). And John began to weep exceedingly, uncontrollably, because no one was found worthy to open the scroll or look into it." John was distraught and cried out that no one anywhere was worthy of taking and opening the scroll. Revelation 5:5 states, "And one of the elders said to John to stop weeping; behold the Lion from the tribe of Judah, the root of David, Jesus has overcome (conquered) so as to open the book and its seven seals."

Why was Jesus the only one found worthy to open the scroll? Because Jesus is from the lineage of the tribe of David and Judah and the infinite power in self-sacrifice. He humbled Himself and was exalted above every name. Jesus was crucified and shed His blood for us, was resurrected, and was the only one qualified to take the scroll.

We read that Jesus was not given the scroll. Jesus took the scroll from God's powerful, authoritative right hand. When Jesus took the scroll, He took the responsibility that came with opening the scroll. "And He, Jesus came, and He took it out of the right hand of Him (God) who sat on the throne" (Revelation 5:7).

The Seven-Sealed Scroll is revealed in chapter six of the Book of Revelation. The opening of the seals starts God's judgment on the unrepentant unbelievers of the world in the Tribulation. Only one seal is broken or opened at a time. The scroll unrolls to the next seal and stops. Events will take place or happen on the earth or in Heaven. Then another seal has to be broken to open and unroll to the next seal.

The Four Horsemen

The Four Horsemen of the Apocalypse is what they are sometimes referred to. Used here, Apocalypse means the complete destruction of the world.

The Four Horsemen of the Apocalypse are *symbolic* and *spiritual*. They give the outline which tells the story of what happens in the Tribulation. The Four Horsemen symbolically portray four disastrous occurrences of conquering, war, famine, and death that take place in the Tribulation. A horse *represents* God's judgment of sin and rebellion. The horse is a *metaphor* for the forces of God to accomplish His purposes.

The Four Horsemen are the first four seals opened in the Seven-Sealed Scroll. The opening of the Seals is the beginning of God's judgment of the unbelievers on the earth in the Tribulation.

1. The first seal opened is in Revelation 6:2, it is the *1st horseman*. It is a white horse, and the rider who sits on the white horse has a bow, and a crown is given to the rider. The rider is the Antichrist, and he has a bow, which is symbolic of violence, and the crown is symbolic

of authority given to the Antichrist by Satan. The Antichrist goes out conquering so that he might take control of the world.

2. The second seal opened is the *2nd horseman*. Another of the same kind of horse as the first horse that came out, a red flame-colored horse whose rider has been given a great sword. The rider is the Antichrist, who is to take peace from the earth. Peace has to exist for peace to be taken out. The red horse and the sword symbolize war, blood, and killing one another. Satan gives his authority to the Antichrist to use the sword to kill (Revelation 6:4).

3. The third seal opened is the *3rd horseman*. A black horse comes, whose rider has a pair of balances or scales in his hand. The scale represents famine. Apostle John hears a quart of wheat for a penny and three quarts of barley for a penny and do not harm the oil and the wine. Some versions of the Bible use the word penny, and others use the word denarius. Either way, a penny or denarius represented a day's wage. This means it will take a day's wage to buy food for one day. A quart of *wheat* is a better quality of food to feed one person. Or buy a lesser quality of food, three quarts of *barley*, for a day's wage that would feed a family. The scales are symbolic of famine and inflation resulting from the conquest and war of the first two seals. Food by measure and weight represents a scarcity of food. This will bring the killing of one another other for food. After a war, there is famine because the food supply suffers. The scripture also shows there are limitations when the angel says do not harm the oil and wine. The oil and wine represent food for the wealthy, and they will stock their shelves, controlled by the Antichrist (Revelation 6:5-6).

4. The fourth seal is opened in Revelation 6:7-8. When the fourth seal is opened, John spiritually sees the 4th *horseman*, a pale, gray, ashen, or green-colored horse. The rider that sits upon the gray horse is named Death, and Hell is following Death. Satan gives them the authority to kill one-fourth of the earth with a sword, famine, plagues, pestilence, and the wild beasts of the earth. This rider on the gray horse is the only rider that is given a name. His name is Death, and he has another horse, Hell following him. Death refers to the great pestilence following the wars and famines of the first three seals. Wild beasts is a metaphor for brutal, savage men, meaning war. Following Death is Hell, and Hell is there to gather the dead.

The Four Horsemen have been revealed. The Four Horsemen give the outline of what unfolds in the Tribulation.

1. The Antichrist is revealed, and he comes to conquer the world.

2. The Antichrist makes war.

3. Famine happens in the world.

4. Death comes, and Hell cleans up.

5. When the fifth seal opens, John sees the souls crying out from under the altar in Heaven. They have been slain or martyred during the Tribulation for receiving their salvation, giving their testimony, preaching the Gospel of Jesus, or speaking that Jesus' Kingdom is coming. The souls ask when God will avenge the people who killed them. They are in Heaven, but they want revenge on earth for their death. This shows that the martyred souls from the Tribulation are aware of what is happening below on the earth in the Tribulation, while they are in Heaven.

Beneath the altar shows they are in Heaven but in a different place from the believers that Jesus took in the Rapture. These under the altar are the ones that became believers during the Tribulation, and they are called the *Tribulation Saints*. These martyred souls are given long white robes, which represent righteousness. They are told to wait a little longer for the number of their fellow brethren that are expected to be killed in the Tribulation. God could have a certain number or specific people to be saved during the Tribulation (Revelation 6:9-11).

6. The sixth seal is the global terror, the earthquakes, the sun, the moon, and the stars. When Jesus breaks this sixth seal, all terror happens on *earth*. Earthquakes occur, the moon darkens, and the stars and showers fall from the sky. All mountains and islands are moved from their place. People try to hide from the terror and say to the rocks and mountains to fall on them. How terrible this will be that they would ask rocks and mountains to fall on them and kill them. What would the earth look like if every mountain and island are moved from its place? (Revelation 6:12-15)

7. The seventh seal opens in Revelation 8:1, and there is silence in Heaven for half an hour. This half an hour of silence is literal. An angel (a special powerful angel that is before the throne) stands at the altar with a golden censer of frankincense (a censer is a vessel to burn incense). The angel is given much incense (incense makes amends for sin), and the angel puts the incense in with the prayers of the Saints. This angel put the prayers of the Saints upon the golden altar of the throne. The smoke of the incense *with* the prayers of the Saints goes up before the presence of God. Then the angel takes the censer of frankincense, fills it with the fire from the altar, and throws it to the earth. This is the warning of the coming Trumpet Judgments. The seven special and powerful angels standing before the throne of God are each given a trumpet to start the next set of the Seven Trumpet Judgments.

The Seven Trumpet Judgments

Events will go from bad to worse for the people in the Tribulation. Chapters eight and nine introduce the Seven Trumpet Judgments. This is in the first three and a half years of the Tribulation when there is still political peace on the earth. But God is sending judgments to get the unbeliever's attention for them to turn from their wicked ways and be saved.

1. In Revelation 8:7, the first trumpet sounds, and there is hail and fire mixed with blood. The hail is thrown to the earth, and a third of the earth, a third of the trees, and all green grass are burned. This could be like a meteor falling to the earth that destroys a third of the earth's green environment.

2. Next, the second trumpet is blown, and something like a great mountain burning with fire is thrown into the sea, and a third of the sea becomes blood, a third of the creatures in the sea die, and a third of the ships are destroyed. With this trumpet, the creatures in the sea die when the sea turns to blood and will cause stench and pollution on the shores. A third of the ships destroyed will affect the trade, commerce, and food supply of those on the earth.

3. The third angel sounds, and a great star falls from Heaven, burning like a torch. It falls on a third of the rivers and the springs of the waters. The name of this star is called Wormwood, it has a bitter taste, and many people will die. A third of the drinking water is contaminated with the bitter taste of Wormwood (Revelation 8:9).

4. The fourth trumpet is blown, and a third of the sun, a third of the moon, and a third of the stars are struck. A third of them will be darkened, a third of the day will not shine, and a third of the moon in the night will not shine. They will lose a third of the daylight and nightlight on the earth, and the angel shouts, "Woe, Woe, Woe." This is known as the three "Woes," because of the remaining blast of the following three trumpets (Revelation 8:12-13).

This is the destruction that takes place after the Four Horsemen.

1. The fifth seal killed a *fourth* of the people on earth.

2. The sixth seal causes earthquakes, and all mountains and islands are moved out of their place.

3. The first trumpet destroys a *third* of the earth, a third of the trees, and all green grass.

4. The second trumpet destroys a *third* of the ships and sea life.

5. The third trumpet contaminates a *third* of the rivers and springs by the star Wormwood.

6. The fourth trumpet darkens a *third* of the sun, moon, and stars.

This is what the people will have experienced up to this point in the Tribulation. The first four trumpets are literal plagues affecting the earth, the seas, rivers, and vegetation. The next three trumpets will deal with the moral and spiritual realms and will introduce the three Woes. Woe means grief, anguish, and affliction. The three Woes are the final judgments God pronounces on the inhabitants of the earth.

5. The fifth trumpet is blown in Revelation 9:1-12. This judgment is a *spiritual attack* on the earth. This is the first Woe. The bottomless pit, known as the Abyss, is opened, and spiritual demons that are in the form of a massive swarm of locusts looking like grasshoppers

are let out of the Abyss. Power is given to the locust by a demon called the Destroyer. These locusts are demons and are only allowed to attack people who do not have God's seal on their foreheads. The 144,000 Witnesses have the seal on their forehead so they will not be harmed. The locusts are not allowed to hurt the grass, trees, or any green thing. The locusts are not allowed to kill the people but are to *torment* them for five months with bites like that of a scorpion. Five months is the life span of a locust. This judgment will be so severe that the people will desire to die but will not be able to. These locusts are powerful and will have a demon, named the Destroyer, leading them. The Destroyer's name in Hebrew is *Abaddon*, and in Greek, his name is *Apollyon*. The first Woe has now passed, and there are two more Woes to follow.

6. The sixth trumpet is the second Woe. Four demonic angels are released that have been bound at the Euphrates River, waiting and prepared for this very time. We know they are demonic angels because demonic angels are the only angels that are bound. The four demonic angels will lead an army of approximately two hundred million demonic spirits to kill <u>one-third</u> of mankind by fire, smoke, and sulfur. The rest of mankind who are not killed, have hardened hearts and do not repent of their spiritual idols or turn from their wicked ways. Hardened hearts mean people cannot see the spiritual realities around them or the ways of God (Revelation 9:13).

The fifth seal killed one-fourth of the people, and now with the sixth trumpet, there is another one-third of mankind killed. More than half of the population on earth have been killed.

Halfway through the Tribulation, the Antichrist will break the peace covenant with Israel and make war against Israel. The Abomination that causes Desolation will take place at this time, in the middle of the Tribulation. This second half or last half of the Tribulation is called the "Great Tribulation" because of the great destruction and wrath that God pours out upon the earth and on the unbelieving people.

This is the destruction that has taken place with the Three Woes.

1. The 1ˢᵗ Woe is in the fifth trumpet judgment. This Woe involves the locust that have the ability to sting and torment the people for five months.

2. The 2ⁿᵈ Woe is in the sixth trumpet judgment. The Woe is the release of the four demonic angels that are bound and the armies of two hundred million that kill one-third of mankind.

3. The 3ʳᵈ Woe is the seventh trumpet judgment. This Woe marks the finishing of God's judgment on sin.

7. The Seventh Trumpet is the last and final Trumpet Judgment and is also the third and final Woe to the earth. <u>The seventh trumpet starts the second half of the Tribulation.</u> The seventh angel sounds, saying that the world's kingdom, which has belonged to Satan, has become the kingdom of our God and Christ, and God will *reign* forever and ever (Revelation 11:15-19). This is not good news for the unbelievers in the Tribulation. The Kingdom is now God's, and God will take His great power and will begin to *reign* in this Seventh Trumpet Judgment.

God now begins to reign. God has finished the judgments of sin on the unbelieving world, and will now release His anger and wrath with full force on the world.

The Seven Bowls of God's Wrath

The **second half of the Tribulation** has started. The next Seven Bowls or Seven Vials of Wrath will be upon the earth. The King James Bible uses the word Vials of Wrath, and the New American Standard Bible uses Bowls of Wrath. The Bowls or Vials of Wrath will be supernatural, harsh, and severe, and the people will know that God is doing this destruction. The Bowls of Wrath will punish those *who worshiped* the *beast* and *his image* and those who took the *mark of the beast*. Apostle John heard from the temple of God for the seven angels to go and pour out the seven bowls of God's wrath into the earth (Revelation 16:1).

The Seven Seals and the Seven Trumpets are judgments of sin. The Seven Bowls are God's Wrath, His anger.

1. The First Bowl is in Revelation 16:2. The angel pours out a bowl into the earth, and it became loathsome (hurtful), malignant (painful), sore (boil) upon all the people who had the mark of the beast and worshiped the beast's image.

2. The second angel pours his bowl out onto the sea. The first angel's bowl went to the earth, and now the second angel's bowl goes to the sea. The sea became blood, and every living thing in the sea dies (Revelation 16:3).

3. In Revelation 16:5, the third angel pours his bowl into the rivers and springs of water, and they became blood. The angel of the waters said, "Righteous are Thou (God), **who is and who was**, O Holy One, because Thou didst judge these things."

Notice something very important in this scripture from the New American Standard Bible. There is no: Who is to come! Why? Because God has now come and has begun to reign.

We have always read "**the One Who is and Who was and <u>Who is to come</u>**."

1. In Revelation 1:4, John says to the seven churches, "who is and who was and who is to come."

2. In Revelation 1:8, God says, "who is and who was and who is to come."

3. In Revelation 4:8, the four living ones continually say, "who is and who was and who is to come."

If you look back to Revelation 11:17 at the seventh trumpet judgment, which starts the second half of the Tribulation, the seventh angel sounds, saying that the world's kingdom which has belonged to Satan, <u>has now become the kingdom of our God and Christ</u>, and <u>God will reign forever and ever</u>. This scripture tells us that God <u>has come</u>! So, there is NO more "<u>Who is to come</u>."

Revelation 16:5, "Righteous are Thou (God), **who is and who was**, O Holy One because Thou didst judge these things." As you can see in the scripture, God is now reigning from Heaven and sending out His wrath in the second half of the Tribulation.

In Revelation 16:4-6 in the third bowl, the angel of the waters told the people in the Tribulation that they had killed God's Saints and His Prophets and that God was pouring out His vengeance on them to have blood to drink. All the seas, oceans, rivers, and springs of water filled with blood, and everything in them has died. There is no drinking water, and imagine the stench of the decaying fish and the smell of blood.

4. The fourth angel pours his bowl upon the *sun*, and the sun scorched the people with fire, with third-degree burns. The people have painful boils, nothing to drink, and are now being scorched. The Bible tells us that unbelievers still curse the name of God (Revelation 16:8).

The first four bowls are poured onto the *people, earth, sea, rivers*, and the *sun*. Next, God goes directly after the Antichrist and the Antichrist's Kingdom with this fifth bowl.

5. The fifth angel pours his bowl upon the beast's throne, and the beast's kingdom and it becomes full of darkness. The people will go into convulsions as they gnaw their tongues because of the pain. They are still dealing with the extreme pain from the sores from the first bowl judgment, and now they will have pain and darkness. Yet they still blaspheme God and will not repent of their actions. The Antichrist and his Kingdom include those with the mark of the beast or his number on them (Revelation 16:10).

6. The sixth bowl has the sixth angel pouring out his bowl upon the Euphrates River, and the water dries up. This is to prepare the way for the armies in the Armageddon War to cross over the dry river.

Next, Apostle John, who is in Heaven, sees three unclean demonic spirits emerge, one each out of Satan, the Antichrist, and the False Prophet. These three demonic spirits go out to persuade the earth's kings, who are not under the Antichrist's control, to cooperate with the Antichrist in the war of Armageddon. The three demonic spirits are to convince the kings that the success of their future lies in the whole earth uniting together to stop Christ from taking over the earth at His Second Coming. The demonic spirits are to persuade the nations to fight against Christ. This helps us to understand how the other nations not under the Antichrist's control are persuaded to fight along with the Antichrist in the battle of Armageddon. This also states a very important fact that there are people that do not have the mark or number of the beast (Revelation 16:12).

7. This seventh bowl in Revelation 16:17-21 is the last and final bowl of wrath. This explains the destruction of the Antichrist's evil empire, Babylon. When this seventh angel pours out his bowl in the air, huge *hailstones*, each about one hundred pounds, fall upon the men who are still blaspheming God. There is the mighty destruction of the earth with a great *earthquake*. The earthquake will destroy the city of Babylon and it will cause the islands and the mountains to disappear from the earth. When the seventh angel pours out his bowl upon the air, and a great voice comes out of the temple from the throne of God, saying, "It is done, it is finished." When a voice comes out of the temple of God in Heaven, there are flashes of lightning, sounds, and peals or ripples of thunder. This is God speaking.

Let us do a recap of God's Seven Bowls of Wrath.

1. The first angel pours out a bowl upon the people that become loathsome sores on the people who have the mark of the beast.

2. In the second bowl the sea becomes thick blood and everything in the sea dies.

3. The rivers and springs turn into blood and there is no drinking water in the third bowl.

4. The fourth bowl is poured upon the sun and scorches the people with fire.

5. The fifth angel pours out the bowl directly upon the Antichrist and His Kingdom and everything turns dark. They gnaw their tongues because of the pain.

6. The sixth bowl dries up the Euphrates River.

7. The seventh bowl explains the destruction of Babylon. The seventh angel pours his bowl into the air and one-hundred-pound hail stones fall on the people. God, says, "It is done, it is finished."

What is God saying when He says "It is done, it is finished." Listed are a few things that are finished:

1. The events of the Tribulation are finished (Revelation 4:1-19:21).

2. The 70th week of Daniel is fulfilled, which is the Tribulation, and it has ended (Daniel 9:27).

3. The second half, the Great Tribulation has ended (Revelation 11:15-19:21).

4. Israel is released from the Gentiles and from Satan (Revelation 12:1-19:21).

5. The worship of the Antichrist ends (Revelation 13:1-18; 19:20).

6. The evil empire of Babylon is destroyed (Revelation 16:17-21).

7. The Antichrist's reign on earth ends, and is finished (Revelation 19:11-21).

8. Satan's reign on the earth is finished (Revelation 19:11-20:3; Isaiah 24:21-22).

9. he Second Coming, the eternal reign of Christ begins (Revelation 19:11-21; 20:1-10).

We have discussed and understand the Four Horsemen. We have seen the destruction on the earth and in the air by the Seven Seals of Judgment, the Seven Trumpet Judgments, and what God does with the Seven Bowls of His Wrath.

A Recap of the Events in the Seven Years of the Tribulation

1. John, the bondservant and writer of Revelation, is spiritually called up to Heaven. He is shown the scenes in Heaven and the things that must take place.

2. A man makes a covenant of peace with Israel for seven years; this man will later be known as the Antichrist.

3. The 144,000 Jewish Witnesses will be on the earth as God's servants and missionaries to witness about Jesus and the Kingdom of Jesus to come. Many people will become believers.

4. The Two Prophets will prophesy for 1,260 days in Jerusalem. They will be killed in Jerusalem by the Antichrist. God will raise them from the dead and take them to Heaven.

5. Jesus opens the Seven Seal Judgments.

6. The Four Horsemen of the Apocalypse are introduced.

7. The Seven Trumpet Judgments are released on the earth.

8. We are introduced to the Tribulation Saints in Heaven, those martyred during the Tribulation.

9. The Antichrist breaks the peace covenant with Israel.

10. In the middle of the Tribulation is the destruction of the temple in Jerusalem, the Abomination of Desolation. The image of the Antichrist will be set up to be worshiped in the Temple.

11. The False Prophet's purpose is to be the religious leader and to convince the people to worship the Antichrist and his image.

12. The second half, or the last three-and-one-half years, is called the Great Tribulation.

13. God begins to reign.

14. God's Seven Bowls of Wrath will be released on earth and the people.

15. The Antichrist and the False Prophet have control of Babylon and the evil empire.

16. We learn about the mark of the Beast, and his number 666.

Chapter Nine

◇◇◇◇

THE SECOND
COMING OF CHRIST

THE GREEK TERM for Jesus' Second Coming is *"Parousia."* *Parousia* also means presence, coming, or arrival. *Parousia* is the future return of Jesus Christ in glory. Glory refers to seeing the beauty of His Spirit. The Second Coming is when Jesus will return to judge humanity and set up His Millennial Kingdom.

Jesus' first coming was two thousand years ago when He was born to a virgin named Mary. Jesus lived a perfect life on this earth. He was crucified for us on the cross and went to Hell to take our sins upon Himself. He was buried (lain in the tomb) and rose again after three days. He ascended to Heaven, and before He left, Jesus promised He would come again to judge the world and gather His people, the believers, for Himself.

Jesus was here before, and we are now waiting on His return. The future return is the Second Coming or the Advent of Christ. Advent means the arrival of a notable person or event. Advent is from the Latin word *adventus*, meaning "coming." Advent is a period of spiritual preparation for the Lord's coming. This Second Coming or Second Advent of Christ will take place at the end of the seven years of Tribulation.

Zechariah 14:4 tells us Jesus will arrive from Heaven at His Second Coming, and His feet will stand on the Mount of Olives. Revelation 19:11-21, states that on the first day of His arrival at His Second Coming, Christ and His armies will set foot on the Mount of Olives to fight the battle of Armageddon. The Mount of Olives is on the east side of the Kidron Valley and looks toward the east side of the city of Jerusalem in Israel.

The Mount of Olives

Read very carefully word by word as Matthew 24:29-31 explains Jesus' glorious Second Coming. The sun will be darkened, the moon will not give its light, and the stars will fall from the sky. All the powers of the Heavens will be shaken. Then, the sign of the Son of Man will appear in the sky. All the tribes of the earth will mourn, and they will see the Son of Man, Jesus, coming on the clouds of the sky with power and great glory. He will send forth His angels with the sound of the shofar, and the angels will gather His elect from the earth. Elect refers to the Jewish people and those that have chosen Jesus Christ as their Savior.

The mountain of Mount Olives will split in half; one side will go north, and the other will go south to make a great valley. The remnant of the people of Israel are told to flee through the great valley of the mountain so they will be safe during the Battle of Armageddon. It is thought that they will flee to the mountains of Petra in Jordan where they will be safe.

The caves in Petra, Jordan

Jesus at His Second Coming:

1. Jesus will come from Heaven sitting on a white horse, and He is called Faithful and True. He judges and makes war (Armageddon) in righteousness. The Saints, the believers in Heaven, the Bride of Christ are with Him (Revelation 19:11).

2. His eyes are a flame of fire, and He has many crowns on his head. He has a name written that no man knew but He, Himself (Revelation 19:12).

3. His name is called the Word of God, and His body is clothed with a vesture dipped in blood, meaning pure and holy (Revelation 19:13).

4. The Saints, which are in Heaven with Him, are clothed in fine, pure linen and follow Him on white horses (Revelation 19:14).

5. On His robe and on His thigh is written the name King of Kings and Lord of Lords (Revelation 19:16).

6. Coming out of His mouth is a sharp sword, the Word of God, to smite and to kill the nations' armies at Armageddon. He shall rule them with a rod of iron, and He will trample in fierceness with the wrath of God (Revelation 19:15).

7. We see from the list that Jesus has many names: He is called Faithful and True, a name no man knows, the Word of God, the King of Kings, and the Lord of Lords.

Jesus tells His disciples in Luke 17:26-30, just as it was in the days of Noah and the days of Lot, so shall it be at His Second Coming. Noah and Lot correlate with the story of the destruction of the spiritual city of Babylon in Revelation chapter 17. Babylon represents the Antichrist's the evil empire in the Tribulation. In the evil empire of Babylon, we see that the unbelievers will be eating, drinking, and carrying on business as usual. They will have the mark of the beast on their hand or forehead, and Jesus' Second Coming will destroy this evil empire in the Battle of Armageddon.

The Battle of Armageddon

Armageddon is a literal war. It will take place in Israel at the end of the Tribulation. There is so much information in books and from educated scholars about the battle of Armageddon. There are theories on who the armies and countries will be, from which direction the troops will arrive, and what will happen in war terms. For our purposes here, I will use scripture to tell us what happens in the Armageddon War, what spiritually happens, and where the scriptures fit in the timeline.

The Battle of Armageddon is when the Antichrist gathers his armies made up of his people, the unbelievers. The Antichrist's and his army's purpose is to kill the Jews and the people of Israel and take control of the world.

The Armageddon war is between the armies of men, but it is a battle between the forces of good and evil. The Armageddon war starts before Jesus makes His appearance at His Second Coming, and then Jesus will end the Armageddon war.

There are many names for the word Armageddon as it relates to where the battle will take place.

1. The Hebrew word Har-Megiddo is then translated to the Greek word Armageddon. Armageddon is also an Aramaic word meaning the Mount of Assembly.

2. Har is the mountain of Mageddon. This is the mountain or the city of Megiddo. It is the ruins of an ancient town that overlooks the Valley Esdraelon. The Valley of Esdraelon, also known as the Valley of Jezreel, and is located in northern Israel.

3. The hill of Megiddo is now an archaeological site.

4. Mount Megiddo is a fascinating site of twenty different cities built on top of one another and was continuously inhabited. Megiddo lies at a strategic junction of the roads running north-south and east-west. Whoever had control of Megiddo had control of one of the major trade routes of the "way of the sea." Virtually every invading army that came through this region fought battles for the control of Megiddo and the Jezreel Valley.

5. The location of the hill of Mount Megiddo is sixty miles north of Jerusalem, overlooking the vast Jezreel Valley. The Valley of Jezreel is a broad valley and is in the critical position between the Euphrates and the Nile Rivers. In the Book of Joel, the valley is called the Valley of Decision.

Mount Megiddo today

6. The size of the Jezreel Valley only measures twenty miles long and ten miles wide, but it is in a very strategic location.

The lush Jezreel Valley today, taken from the top of Mount Megiddo

In the prophecy from Daniel in the Old Testament, Daniel informs us about the war of Armageddon. Daniel 11:44 says, "But rumors from the east and from the north will disturb him (the Antichrist), and he will go forth with great wrath to destroy many and annihilate many."

Israel is the target of the Armageddon attacks by the Antichrist. In the final battle, Christ will return with His Church Saints to save Israel and complete the unity of God's people.

John <u>spiritually</u> describes the Armageddon army and its impact on the earth. John states, "And this is how I, John saw in the vision the horses and those who sat on them; the riders had breastplates the color of fire, of hyacinth (blue), and brimstone (sulfur); and the heads of the horses are like the heads of lions, and out of the horse's mouths proceeded fire and smoke and brimstone (demonic forces). A third of mankind was killed by these three plagues, the fire and smoke, and the brimstone which proceeded out of the horse's mouths. For the power (the strength) of the horses is in their mouths and in their tails; for their tails are like serpents and have heads, and with them, they do harm" (Revelation 9:17-19).

Remember from our earlier study that horses represent God's judgments on sin and rebellion. The horse is also a metaphor for the forces of God to accomplish His purposes.

The army of two hundred million in Revelation chapter nine is a literal war but is also a spiritual war. The scripture refers to a massive demonic army that will be unleashed to wreak havoc on the earth.

Many prophecy scholars believe that the most reasonable explanation of this prophecy relates to the great Euphrates River. The army rises from the far East and crosses the Euphrates River to participate in the final war of Armageddon. The reference to a vast army and the Euphrates River is often correlated with Revelation chapter sixteen, which also mentions "the kings of the east" and the Euphrates River.

The understanding of "the kings from the east" is to take the passage literally. The kings of the east refer to the nations who are from the east of the Euphrates. Genesis 15:18 points to the Euphrates River as the eastern boundary of the land promised to Abraham and his descendants, the nation of Israel.

Revelation 16:14 describes, "For they (Satan, Antichrist, and False Prophet) are spirits of demons, performing signs which go out to the kings of the whole world, to gathering them (the kings) together for the war of the great day of God the Almighty." Again, in Revelation 16:16, "And the evil spirits gather the rulers and the armies together to the place which in Hebrew is called *Har-Magedon*." This reveals that the focal point of the gathering is Armageddon and the reference to Mount Megiddo.

The great armies from the east and the west will gather and assemble on this Valley of Jezreel around the hill of Megiddo. The Antichrist's purpose is to gather the armies of the world to execute what the Antichrist thinks is the final solution to the Jewish problem. Jesus Christ will return to prevent the Antichrist's purpose and his attempt to annihilate or destroy the Jewish people.

The devastation of Armageddon will be so extensive that it will destroy most of the earth. The plant life will be nearly eliminated, and the air and water will be severely polluted. The carnage, the killing of many people, will be great. The armies of the Antichrist will be wiped out, and all the birds will be filled with their flesh. "And from His (Jesus) mouth comes a sharp sword (the Word), so that with it He may smite the nations" (Revelation 19:15). Jesus speaks, and the battle is over!

In Revelation 19:17-19, John sees an angel standing in the sun. The angel cried out with a loud voice, saying to all the birds flying in the air to come and assemble for the "great supper" that will be provided for the birds by God. The angel will call together the birds to eat and be filled with the flesh of those who were killed in battle.

The death toll is so extensive that it includes the kings, commanders, mighty men, and the flesh of horses. As the Antichrist and his armies approach Jerusalem, God will intervene, and The Lord and His angelic army will destroy the armies and capture the Antichrist and the False Prophet.

Revelation 19:20 tells us what happens to the beast known as the Antichrist and the False Prophet. "And the beast (Antichrist) was seized, and with him, the false prophet who performed the signs in his presence by which he (False Prophet) deceived those who had received the mark of the beast and those who worshiped his image; these two were <u>thrown alive</u> <u>into the lake of fire</u> which burns with brimstone."

"And the rest were killed with the sword (Word) which came from the mouth of Him (Jesus) who sat upon the horse, and all the birds were filled with their flesh (great supper)." The armies will be killed with the Word that comes out of the mouth of Jesus (Revelation 19:21).

We know a literal sword does not come out of the mouth of Jesus. This is a metaphor meaning the Word of God. The Word of God comes out of Jesus's mouth and destroys the armies. The War of Armageddon is over, and God throws the Antichrist and the False Prophet alive into the Lake of Fire.

There will be Jewish and non-Jewish people that have survived to the end of the Tribulation. We will learn more about what happens to the people who live through the Tribulation.

The Parable of the Sheep and Goat Judgment

The Sheep and Goat Judgment takes place after the Tribulation. The Sheep and Goat Judgment is the judgment of the gentile non-Jewish nations that survived the Tribulation. (Nations are defined as a large body of people united by common descent, history, culture, or language inhibiting a particular country or territory). The Sheep represents the compassionate gentile non-Jewish people, and the goats the hard-hearted people. Jesus will separate the gentiles on how they treated the Jewish people during the Tribulation. Did they help the Jewish people, or did they turn a blind eye to the Jews' troubles? Or did they help the other gentiles in the persecution of the Jews during the Tribulation?

In Matthew 25:31-46 Jesus explains to His disciples the parable of the Sheep and Goat Judgment "But when the Son of Man comes in His glory (the Second Coming), and all the angels with Him, then Jesus will sit on His glorious throne, and all the nations will be gathered before Him, and He will separate them from one another as the shepherd separates the sheep from the goats, and Jesus will put the sheep on His right, and the goats on the left" (Matthew 25:31-32). The gentile nations are gathered for judgment to determine who is worthy of going into the Millennial Kingdom and who will get death for the mistreatment of Israel.

Jesus speaks to the gentile nations about their treatment of Israel. "For I was hungry, and you gave Me something to eat; I was thirsty, and you gave Me drink; I was a stranger, and you invited Me in; naked, and you clothed Me; I was in prison, and you came to Me" (Matthew 25:35-36).

"Then the righteous (the sheep, the compassionate gentiles) will answer Him, saying, Lord, when did we give You drink? And when did we see you a stranger, and invite you in, or naked and clothe you? And when did we see you sick, or in prison, and come to you?" (Matthew 25:37-39) "And the King (King used in this scripture is Jesus the Messiah who is often called King, King of Israel or King of the Jews) will answer and say to them, Truly I say to you (the righteous, sheep) to the extent that you did it to one of these brothers of Mine, even the least of them, you did it to Me" (Matthew 25:40).

To the goats, the hard-hearted people, "He (Jesus) will say to those on His left, depart from Me, accursed ones (doomed or detestable), into the eternal fire which has been prepared for the devil and his angels" (the Lake of Fire). Then Jesus will explain to them, "For I was hungry, and you gave Me nothing to eat; I was thirsty, and you gave Me nothing to drink; I was a stranger, and you did not invite Me in; naked, and you did not clothe Me; sick, and in prison, and you did not visit Me" (Matthew 25:42-43).

"Then they (accursed ones, goats) themselves also will answer saying, Lord, when did we see You hungry, or thirsty, or a stranger, or naked, or sick, or in prison, and did not take care of You?" (Matthew 25:44)

Jesus will answer them and explain by saying, "Truly I say to you, to the extent that you did not do it to one of the least of these, you did not do it to Me. And these (the accursed ones) will go away into eternal punishment (Lake of Fire), but the righteous into eternal life" (Matthew 25:45-46).

This is the separation of the Sheep and Goat Judgment of the gentile nations who survived the Tribulation. This judgment aims to determine which gentiles will enter the Millennial Kingdom and which will go into the Lake of Fire.

Jesus will say to the sheep on His right, my Father has blessed you, and you will enter the Millennial Kingdom. "Come, you are blessed by my Father, inherit the Kingdom prepared for you from the foundation of the world" (Matthew 25:34).

Jesus continues by saying to those on His left, the goats, the accursed ones, those that mistreated Israel. "Depart from me, you are cursed into the lake of fire." They survived the Tribulation, are judged by Jesus, and are sent to the Lake of Fire for Eternity.

After the Separation of the Sheep and Goat Judgment, we will learn from scripture that there are extra days added in the Tribulation.

Seventy-Five Days to be Accounted For

There will be seventy-five days to be accounted for between Jesus' Second Coming at the end of the Tribulation and the start of the Millennial Kingdom. There are 1,260 days in each half of the Tribulation which totals 2,520 and equals the seven years.

The Jewish people will make daily sacrifices in the temple in Jerusalem during the first half of the Tribulation. This is the Jewish law for atonement and sanctification for sin. In the middle of the Tribulation, the Antichrist will abolish the continual burnt-offering, destroy the temple, and set an image of himself in the temple to be worshiped, known as the Abomination of Desolation.

We know from the scriptures that there will be thirty extra days added in the first half of the Tribulation. The scripture for the additional thirty days is in Daniel 12:11, "And from the time that the regular sacrifice is abolished, and the Abomination of Desolation is set up, there will be 1,290 days." There are 1,260 in the first half of the Tribulation, and this scripture tells us there will be 1,290 days. This is thirty extra days to be accounted for. We are not informed as to where these thirty extra days are used or what they are used for.

We also know an extra forty-five days will be added in the second half of the Tribulation to make 1,335 days. Daniel 12:12 states, "How blessed is he who keeps waiting and attains to the 1335 days." These 1,335 days are forty-five more days added to the thirty days to account for seventy-five extra days in the second half of the Tribulation. The one who lives forty- five days to 1,335 days is called blessed.

Many things will happen during the extra forty-five days in the second half of the Tribulation. Think of this time as similar to the Presidential election in November and the inauguration in January, a time of preparation.

Some of the events that will occur during the forty-five days in preparation for the Millennium to start are:

1. Jesus will send angels to gather all the people hidden in the hills and caves.
2. The land of Israel will need to be cleansed of debris and machinery after the war of Armageddon.
3. The Temple will have been demolished and will need to be cleaned and rebuilt.
4. The gentile nations of people that lived to the end of the Tribulation will be judged. This is the separation of the Sheep and Goat Judgment.
5. Jesus will cast the Antichrist and the False Prophet into the Lake of Fire.
6. Satan is bound and will be thrown into the abyss for 1,000 years.
7. The Tribulation believers that died and are in Heaven will be resurrected in glorious bodies to rule and reign in the Millennial Kingdom (Revelation 20:4).
8. God will assign responsibilities for the administration of His Millennial Kingdom. He will establish and appoint those aiding in the government of His Kingdom.
9. The descendants of the tribes of Israel will be settled in their portions of land in Israel.

The Millennium will begin after the seventy-five-day interval from the 1,260 days for the second half of the Tribulation to the 1,335 days spoken about in Daniel. The Millennial Kingdom will be on the cleansed earth where the one thousand years with Jesus will begin. Jesus will take His throne, and the believers, the Saints, will rule and reign with Him over the nations.

In Jerusalem, the system of government order and organization of the nations in the Millennial Kingdom will begin, and it will last for one thousand years, as spoken of in Revelation 20:3, 5-6.

Israel's Regathering and Return

Have you ever wondered when Israel will repent and be regathered back to the Lord? Isaiah 66:7-8 indicates that the salvation of men at the Second Coming of Christ refers to Israel. Isaiah refers to the remnant of Israel, the people left in Israel after the Armageddon War. By the time of Armageddon and Christ's return, two-thirds of Israel will be destroyed. Zechariah 12:10-13 tells us this will be when Israel shows great repentance. This will be their great conversion at the Second Coming of the Messiah. Zechariah 12:10 describes to us that Jesus will pour out the Spirit of Grace and supplication on the inhabitants of Jerusalem. Israel will look upon Jesus whom they pierced, and they will mourn and weep bitterly over Him. This scripture identifies the Jews and Israel as the ones responsible for the suffering and death of the Messiah, having been the ones who pierced Him or had Him pierced. Then Israel will weep bitterly and mourn in bitterness over what the Jews did when they see Jesus the Messiah and the marks of His wounds at His Second Coming. They will, at last, ask for mercy and forgiveness from Jesus.

Zechariah tells us two parts of Israel will be destroyed in the Tribulation, leaving only one-third to be preserved alive. This one-third will make up the nation that will be saved in a day at the Second Coming of Christ.

"And it will come about in all the land, that two parts in it will be cut off and perish. But the third will be left in it, and I will bring the third part through the fire, refine and test them. They will call on My name, and I will answer them. I will say they are My people, and they will say, The Lord is my God" (Zechariah 13:8-9).

The Day of the Lord begins with the Second Coming of Christ the Messiah and lasts to the end of the Millennium when the Day of God begins and continues through Eternity. The Second Coming of Christ will fulfill the prophecy of Joel 2:28. "I will pour out My Spirit on all mankind." Acts 2:16-21 also verified by Peter that the Spirit will be poured out upon mankind in the last days.

Romans 11:25 explains that the secret or mystery is that a partial hardening of the hearts and blindness has happened to Israel. This is there until the fullness of the Gentiles, the non-Jews, has come in full (been saved). Then all of Israel will be saved. The hardening of the hearts and blindness means being spiritually lost and unable to see God's truth. This blindness and partial hardening of the hearts is in place until Christ's Second Coming. Then Israel will have a national conversion that will end Israel's rebellion. At the battle of Armageddon, a tremendous outpouring of the Holy Spirit will take place on Israel, and the hardening of their hearts and blindness to God's Word will be lifted from them.

Deuteronomy 30:1-10 tells us of Israel's regather and Israel's return. Then Israel is converted and turns to God with their whole heart and soul. Only a partial regathering of Israel will occur before the Second Coming of Christ. The final and complete regathering will be at the Second Coming and after that until all are gathered from every part of the earth (Isaiah 11:10-12; Matthew 24:29-31).

"Then the Lord your God will restore you (Israel) from captivity and have compassion on you and will gather you again, from all the peoples where the Lord your God has scattered you (at the Second Coming regathering). If your outcasts are at the ends of the earth, from there, the Lord will gather you, and from there, He will bring you back. And the

Lord your God will bring you into the land which your fathers (Abraham, Isaac, and Jacob) possessed, and you shall possess it (in the Millennium). And God will prosper you and multiply you more than your fathers (Patriarchs)" (Deuteronomy 30:3).

Matthew 24:30-31: "The sign of the Son of Man (at the Second Coming) will appear in the sky, and then all the tribes of the earth will mourn, and they will see the Son of Man coming." They will realize Jesus is the Son of God, and their ancestors had persecuted Jesus, and they will mourn. "And Jesus will send forth His angels with a great sound of the shofar, and the angels will gather together His elect (His people, Israel) from one end of the earth to the other." These scriptures refer to the return of Jesus at His Second Coming, but it is also the repentance of the chosen people, the Jews, and the regathering of Israel.

Chapter Ten

◇◇◇◇

THE MILLENNIAL KINGDOM

THE LATIN PHRASE *mille* is a thousand, and *annus* is a year. The one-thousand years of the Millennium are known as the Millennial Kingdom or Jesus' Millennial Reign. The direct administration of divine government by Jesus will take place in Jerusalem on this earth where Israel is today. More land will be added to increase the size of present-day Israel for the Millennial Kingdom.

The Saints that have been in Heaven with Jesus, will live in the Millennial Kingdom for one thousand years, and they will rule and reign with Jesus.

Isaiah 9:6-7 states, "For a child (Jesus) will be born to us, a son will be given to us, and the <u>government will rest on His shoulders</u>; and His name will be called Wonderful, Counselor, Mighty God, Eternal Father, Prince of Peace. There will be no end to the increase of His government or of peace."

Isaiah is talking about Jesus in the Millennial Kingdom, the government will be upon Jesus, and His responsibility is to govern the Kingdom. The ruling, the authority, the judgment, and justice will be Jesus' responsibility in the Millennial Kingdom.

If you consider there will be <u>two groups</u> of people entering the Millennium, it will be easier to understand. I like to use the term the *Natural people* and the *Resurrected* people, meaning the people in natural earthly bodies and those in resurrected bodies.

The natural people are the people who lived through and come out of the Tribulation. They will enter the Millennial Kingdom and be known as the nations. Nations is translated from the Greek word ethnos. This is a particular group or race of people. The nations, the natural people, will have their natural earthly bodies, as they did during the Tribulation. They will marry and have children during the Millennium.

The resurrected people are the Saints that have been in Heaven during the time of the Tribulation. They will have the same resurrected bodies they had in Heaven, the same resurrected body that Jesus has. They will rule and reign with Jesus over the natural people of the nations in the Millennium.

The Natural People of the Nations

There will be people, both saved and unsaved, Jews and non-Jews entering the Millennium. They lived through the Tribulation's judgments, God's wrath, and Armageddon, and did not take the mark of the Antichrist. I referred earlier in our study to these people and to the Kings of the armies that had not followed the Antichrist and said we would learn more about them. They are the natural people in the Millennium.

All the kingdoms will become the Kingdom of our Lord. No scripture hints that these kingdoms will be made up entirely of saved people. Salvation is not a requirement for continuing to live on the earth after Jesus sets up His Millennial Kingdom.

The people that lived through the Tribulation and through the Sheep and Goat Judgment will need to be cared for and healed mentally and physically. The Millennium is a time of refinement for the people of the nations.

The regathering will continue in the Millennium. The resurrected Saints and earthly believers will be sent out from Jerusalem to preach the gospel to everyone, including unbelievers brought into the Millennium from the Tribulation. The earthly believers will take over all parts of the earth until the whole is brought under the subjection of Christ. How fast and with what immediate success the Kingdom of Christ will extend over the entire world is unknown.

If the natural people of the nations did not take the mark of the beast, if they did not persecute the Jews during the Tribulation, and if they are otherwise worthy of entrance into the Kingdom, they will be left on the earth to live as natural people in the Millennium. But they will be required to go up or at least send a representative to Jerusalem to worship Jesus and to keep the Feast of Tabernacles yearly. If they do not go up as required, there will be no rain upon their land.

Zechariah 14:16: "Then it will come about that any who are left of all the nations that fought against Jerusalem in the Armageddon war with the Antichrist will go up from year to year to worship the King, the Lord of Host, and to celebrate the Feat of the Tabernacles."

It is plainly stated in Isaiah that many in the Millennium will hear of Christ and His reign in Jerusalem. Isaiah 2:2, "Now it will come about that in the last days, the mountain of the house of the Lord will be established as the chief of the mountains, and will be raised above the hills, and all the nations will stream to it."

Isaiah 2:3, and may peoples will come and say, "Come and let us go up to the mountain of the Lord, to the house of the God of Jacob; and He will teach us of His ways, and we will walk in His paths. For out of Zion (Jerusalem) will go forth the law, civil laws of the government, the Word of the Lord, and the gospel. And the Messiah shall judge among many nations and shall rebuke many people." Isaiah 2:4, "And He will judge between the nations and will render decisions for many peoples."

Why would He need to judge and rebuke if all were believers and already submitted to Him? The Word of the Lord will go out from Jerusalem, and salvation will be offered to all people in the Millennium (Isaiah 52:7).

The Millennial Kingdom will be a literal, physical, and visible Kingdom in Israel. The people of the nations will have earthly bodies, and they will marry and have children. Under the perfect conditions of the Millennium, the nations will quickly multiply as multitudes of children are born to populate the Kingdom.

"The natural people, the nations shall build houses and inhabit them, they will plant vineyards and eat their fruit, they shall not build a house, and another inhabit it, they shall not plant, and another eat" (Isaiah 65:21-22). They will enjoy doing their work. They will grow and eat their own food. Everyone will have their own homes, as stated in scripture. They will not live in a house that someone else built or had lived in before them like we do today.

Cities will be rebuilt, and the population on earth in the Millennium will grow as the conditions will be favorable, and the curse of hard labor will be removed. With the change in purpose and production of material goods, God's blessing will be upon all labor and business. Nothing will be produced for war.

"For the youth will die at the age of one hundred, and the one who does not reach the age of one hundred shall be thought accursed" (Isiah 65:20). Accursed means doomed, ill-fated, and wretched.

"They shall not labor in vain, or bear children for calamity; for they are the offspring of those blessed by the Lord, and their descendants with them." Calamity in Greek means doomed for terror. The children will be the offspring of those blessed by the Lord when they are born in the Millennium. No longer will there be an infant who lives only a few days, nor an older man who does not live out his days (Isaiah 65:23).

Children born during the Millennial Kingdom will be responsible for their own faith and salvation in Christ, as all people of past ages have been. They will still have a free will, just as it is for us now. Whether we receive Jesus as our Lord and Savior is our choice. That decision will also be the children's choice if they accept Jesus and serve Him. The children will be born to believers, but they must make their own decisions to believe in Jesus. In the Millennial thousand years, there will be many generations born.

As the generations descend further and further from the first believers, more people will fall away from the truth of Jesus, even under the blessed conditions they will live in.

The nations will have human life that will be prolonged if they obey the laws in the Millennium. Those who commit sins that require the death penalty will be executed. Death will continue throughout the Millennium for the natural people, the nations. Any rebellion will not last long, Jesus, who is in charge, will know the intent of every heart, and there will be swift justice for every wrong. The Lord will rule with a rod of iron (Revelation 2:27) which means there will not be any long delays in justice, no trials, and no waiting for sentences to be carried out. There will be immediate justice based upon the holy reign of Jesus. If a person at any age, whether one hundred or five hundred years old, commits a sin, he will receive the death penalty and be executed. The law will go forth from Jerusalem by Jesus.

"It will also come to pass that before they call (the natural people), Jesus will answer; and while they are still speaking, I/Jesus will hear" (Isaiah 65:24). This would indicate that prayer will continue in the Millennium. Isaiah 65:25 informs us that the curse in Genesis will be lifted in the Millennium, and the wolf and the lamb shall feed together, the lion, a meat- eater, shall eat straw like the ox, and the serpent's meal will be dust. In the Millennium, the snakes will lose their poisonous fangs, they shall do no harm. With the changes in animal nature and society, the animals will not hurt or destroy anything in the Kingdom. The earth will be in true harmony.

From this scripture, we know there will be animals in the Millennium.

God's greater purpose for the Millennium is for Jesus to prepare the natural people to enter Eternity. The nations, the natural people, will need to be spiritually cleansed and prepared to enter the purity and the Holiness of God and Eternity.

The Resurrected Believers

The believers in Heaven will enter the Millennial Kingdom fully reigned by Jesus and His government. The resurrected believers will openly love and worship Jesus. Each believer will have opportunities to serve the Lord based on their faithfulness in serving Him now in His Kingdom on earth.

We have studied the rewards and crowns that the believers will receive in Heaven at the Judgment Seat of Christ. The rewards the believers receive will carry over into the Millennium. They will be used to find the believers serving positions in the Millennium. Many will be teaching the Word of God to the natural people. There will be serving, leadership, and government positions for the believer. All the believers will have things to do and roles to fill to serve with Jesus.

Revelation 5:10 states, "And Thou hast made them to be a kingdom and priest to our God. And they will reign upon the earth." The resurrected believers from Heaven will have a part in the administration of the Millennial Kingdom. The believers will be kings and priests when Christ comes to reign. 2 Timothy 2:11 reassures us, "If we die with Jesus, we shall also live with Him." That is our salvation. If we endure and keep ourselves focused on Him, we shall also reign with Him.

Revelation 2:26-27 is essential for us to understand. Jesus is telling the church, "And he (believer) who overcomes and he who keeps My (Jesus) deeds until the end, to him I will give authority over the nations; and he (believer) shall rule them (nations) with a rod of iron, as I also have received authority from My Father." The believers will rule and reign with Jesus over the nations, the natural people, in the Millennial Kingdom. Reigning is defined as possessing or exercising sovereign power and authority to rule, to be predominant or prevalent, and to exercise power or authority. Synonyms for reign are prevailing, governing, authoritative, and administer.

1 Corinthians 15:24-27 is such a good scripture: "Then comes the end (the Millennium) when Jesus delivers up His Millennial Kingdom to God the Father when Jesus has abolished all rule and all authority and power (Satan). For Jesus must reign until He has put all of His enemies under His feet. The last enemy that will be abolished is death and sin. For Jesus has put all things (Satan the last enemy) in subjection under His feet."

Satan's One Last Battle

Unfortunately, not all the people born during the Millennial Kingdom will come to faith in Christ. John tells us that when the thousand years of the Millennium are completed, Satan will be released from the prison of the Abyss, where he has been kept for the last one thousand years. Satan was thrown into the Abyss at the end of the Tribulation (Revelation 20:7-10).

The Abyss was not created for man. God created the Abyss for Satan, his angels, and demons. Satan, his angels, and demonic forces will be released from the Abyss to go throughout the earth. At the last of the Millennium, Satan will go out to deceive the unbelieving people of the nations. No weapons or war training will have occurred in the Millennium, and Satan will deceive the nations into believing they can take over the Saints and Jerusalem without weapons. This one final, unsuccessful rebellion proves many unbelievers will exist during the Millennium's last days. Revelation 20:8 reads, "The number of the unbelieving nation, the people, is like that of the sand on the seashore."

Satan and the unbelievers, which number like the sand on the seashore, will come up on the broad plain of the earth and surround the camp of the Saints and the city of Jerusalem. Then fire will come down from God and devour Satan and the unbelievers. This will be the last rebellion of Satan and the unbelieving people against God and Christ (Revelation 20:9).

This will officially end all rebellion on earth. Satan and the unbelieving people will all be thrown alive into the Lake of Fire for Eternity. Already in the Lake of Fire are the Antichrist and the False Prophet, having been sent there at the end of the Tribulation by Jesus at His Second Coming. Also the unbelievers, the goats from the Sheep and Goat Judgment were sent there by Jesus at the end of the Tribulation. Now Satan and the unbelievers out of the Millennium are sent to the Lake of Fire.

God will now deal with the unbelievers that have been held in Hell. The unbelievers that died while living on the earth from all times past, including the unbelievers that died in the Tribulation, will have gone to Hell. As we know, Hell is a temporary holding place for the unbelievers until they will be sent to their final destination in the Lake of Fire.

The Great White Throne Judgment

As I have previously stated, Hades and Hell are considered the same place. Hades is the Greek word for Hell. From the beginning of time, the unrighteous, the sinner, the idolator, and the murderers have been sent to Hades. The New Testament commonly uses the term, Hell. In the New Testament, all sinners and the ungodly who die without Jesus go to Hell. Hell is their holding place. Many think of Hell as the unbeliever's final destination, but as we have learned, it is not!

There will be one last great judgment of the unbelieving people that have been held in Hell. This is the Great White Throne Judgment. In Revelation 20:11-15, Apostle John saw those standing before the Great White Throne. They were spiritually dead, meaning separated from God. John saw the sinners, the great, the prosperous, the famous, and the small, all standing there waiting on judgment.

The Great White Throne Judgement takes place after the Millennium. Revelation 20:13 informs us, "And the sea gave up the dead which was in it, and death and Hades gave up the dead which was in them, and they were judged, every one of them according to their deeds (sins)." This scripture is packed full of information. It shows that no matter when or where an unbeliever dies, the unbeliever will go to Hell. This scripture also states that they will be judged according to their deeds or the sins they committed while on earth. This states there are different degrees of torment according to the sins they commented while on the earth.

Those in Hades/Hell will be brought before the Great White Throne Judgment. The books will be opened.

We do know one of the books that will be opened is the Book of Life. The unbeliever will know their name is not written in the Book of Life. "If anyone's name was not found written in the book of life, he was thrown into the Lake of Fire" (Revelation 20:15).

The Great White Throne Judgment is an individual judgment, and each sinner will stand before God for a personal judgment of their sins. More than one book will be opened. I believe the books opened will have each sinner's name recorded in them. The books will list what each sinner did, the degree of their sin, and why they are sent to the Lake of Fire. They will have their sins judged according to the books. I believe the worse the evil they committed on earth, the worse the torment will be in the Lake of Fire.

Their Eternity in the Lake of Fire is their second death. The sinner died a physical death once on earth and was sent to Hell. Now they will die their "second death, their spiritual death," and go to the Lake of Fire. The Lake of Fire is described as a place of fire, hot with sulfur and brimstone, it is a never-ending torment, and they can never escape from it. This is not death, they will not die, this is the torment of the wicked, day and night without ever ceasing, a total separation from God and anything good.

Chapter Eleven

◇◇◇◇

THE BOOK OF LIFE

THERE IS A difference between The Book of Life and The Lamb's Book of Life.

The Book of Life is God's book, the role, the list made before the beginning of time of all those that will be saved. It contains all the names of those who will live forever with God in Eternity.

The believer's name and the days of his life are recorded in The Book of Life. This book shows God's knowledge and plans for our life even before we were born. In Psalm 139, God tells us He knew about us before the beginning of time, wrote our name, and recorded all the days ordained for each of us in The Book of Life.

Psalm 139:4: "Even before there is a word on my tongue, behold, O Lord, thou dost know it all."

Psalm 139:14: "I will give thanks to Thee for I am fearfully and wonderfully made."

Psalm 139:16: "Thine eyes have seen my unformed substance; and in thy book they were all written, the days that were ordained for me, when as yet there was not one of them."

God's people already have their name written in God's Book of Life, the register of the Old and New Testaments believers, the Saints who have eternal life with God.

A person's name could be removed or blotted out of the Book of Life in the Old Testament. This removal of one's name was possible in the

Old Testament because of sin and idolatry. God is talking to the idolater in Deuteronomy 29:20. "The Lord shall never be willing to forgive him, but rather the anger of the Lord and His jealousy will burn against that man, and every curse which is written in this book will rest on him (the idolater), and the Lord shall blot out his name from under Heaven."

"May they, David's enemies, be blotted out of the book of life, and may they not be recorded with the righteous" (Psalm 69:28).

God replied to Moses, "Whoever has sinned against me, I will blot out of My book" (Exodus 32:33).

God keeps excellent records, He knows His own, and has set the names of His children in His Book.

The Lamb's Book of Life

The Lamb's Book of Life is a book of salvation. The believers who receive their salvation through Jesus Christ are also written in the Lamb's Book of Life. The scripture in the New Testament states, "And nothing unclean and no one who practices abomination and lying shall ever come into the New Jerusalem (in Eternity), but only those whose names are written in The Lamb's Book of Life" (Revelation 21:27).

The Lamb's Book of Life started with the New Testament. When a person becomes a believer and is saved through the blood of Jesus Christ, their name is written in the Lamb's Book of Life.

God's Book of Life can contain all of The Lamb's Book of Life, but The Lamb's book of Life does not contain all of The Book of Life. The Book of Life is from the beginning of time to the end. The Lamb's Book of Life is for those who received salvation through Jesus Christ.

Can one's name be blotted out of the Lamb's Book of Life? Revelation 3:5 tells us this is the promise "He who overcomes shall thus be clothed in white garments, and I will not erase his name from the book of life." Not only that, but the scripture goes on to say, "And I will confess his name before My Father and before His angels. I give eternal life to them, and they shall never perish, and no one shall snatch (to seize or take by force) them out of my hand. My Father, who has given them to Me, is greater than all; and no one is able to snatch them out of the Father's hand. I and the Father are one" (John 10:28-30). No true believer should ever doubt his eternal security in Christ Jesus.

No scripture in the New Testament refers to being removed or blotted out of the Lamb's Book of Life. Several scriptures state that no one will be allowed into Heaven or Eternity if their name is not written in the Lamb's Book of Life.

Can one be saved, then lose their salvation? That is a question that only Jesus can and will answer. What about the statement once saved, always saved? That is another question that only Jesus can and will answer.

The Book of Remembrance

There is also a Book of Remembrance that the Lord wrote to His faithful believers in the Old Testament. The Lord heard the believers talking to each other, wondering if the Lord would remember them. The Lord wrote to reassure the believers that they were remembered.

"Then those (the Old Testament believers) who feared the Lord, spoke to one another, and the Lord listened and heard them; so, a book of remembrance was written before Him for those who fear the Lord and who meditate on His name" (Malachi 3:16 NKJ). This book assured the Old Testament believers that the Lord would remember them.

Chapter Twelve

◇◇◇◇

ETERNITY

Why will God Destroy the Old Heaven and the Old Earth?

GOD WILL DESTROY the first two Heavens filled with evil where Satan lives. But He will not destroy the third Heaven where God dwells. Ephesians tells us Satan is the god of this dark world, and his helpers perform spiritual wickedness in heavenly realms. Therefore, after the final rebellion of Satan at the end of the Millennium, God will destroy this present earth by fire that is marred and cursed by Satan's evil. God will destroy the first two heavens to guarantee that all evil has been destroyed. As we know it today, this present creation, the earth, will be destroyed by fire from all the effects of Satan, his angels, and sin. This will make way for the New Heaven and the New Earth.

"But the present heavens and earth by His word are being reserved for fire, kept for the day of judgment and destruction of ungodly men" (2 Peter 3:7).

"But the day of the Lord will come like a thief, in which the heavens will pass away with a roar and the elements (physical world) will be destroyed with intense heat (fire), and the earth and its works will be burned up" (2 Peter 3:10).

The New Heaven and the New Earth

The New Heaven and New Earth begin with Gods people living with Him in the new city, New Jerusalem. Eternity is the destination for Gods people, where God will dwell among His people, and we, the believers, will see Him face to face.

The New Heaven and the New Earth is a literal physical place where we, the believer, will dwell in our glorified and resurrected bodies. We will experience a new and perfect place where we will dwell forever.

In the Book of Revelation, Apostle John says, "I saw," reminding us again that John's revelation is a vision of future events in the vocabulary, language, and descriptive terms of Apostle John's time. What he sees is a real place, a city, with a wall around the city, and the wall has gates. There are inhabitants, a place of great activity, worship, and service to God, and it will be our eternal home.

The Measurements of the City, New Jerusalem

Many have tried to explain what they think New Jerusalem will look like. They have called New Jerusalem a square or a cube. I want to explain what I believe New Jerusalem will look like. I am basing my information on going to Eternity, seeing New Jerusalem, and carefully studying the scriptures in the Book of Revelation.

The King James Bible converts the wall's length and the city's width to roughly 1,400 miles. The New American Standard Bible converts it to approximately 1,500 miles. I will use 1,500 miles for reference.

This is what Revelation 21:15-17 tells us about the measurements. The city is in the form of a square, and the wall around the city is also in the form of a square. The city itself is a square within the square wall. Each side of the city base is the length of 1,500 miles. The city inside the wall is a mountain on which we will live, and the mountain is 1,500 miles high or tall. The wall has a length of 1,500 miles on each side, making a square, and the mountain of the city is 1,500 miles tall. This is where New Jerusalem as a cube comes from. I do not believe we will view New Jerusalem as a cube because the city mountain is higher than the walls and looks out over the walls.

The wall is a square around the square city. This could explain how there are different measurements. The square wall would have to be a little larger to engulf the square city. If one of the walls were flipped and stood on its end at the cornerstone, the wall would be as tall as the height of the mountain of the city because the length of the wall is the same as the height of the city.

In Revelation 21:15, the angel spoke with John, and the angel had a gold measuring rod or reed to measure three things. 1. the city, 2. the wall, and 3. the gates. The city and the wall are two different places to be measured.

Revelation 21:16 tells us, "The city itself is laid out as a square (1,500 miles), and its length is as great as its width; and he measured the city with the rod, 1,500 miles; its length and width and height are equal."

New Jerusalem of 1,500 miles would be about the size of measuring from the Canadian border to the Gulf of Mexico and from the great lakes to California.

"The angel measured its wall seventy-two yards, according to human measurements, which are also angelic measurements" (Revelation 21:17). The seventy-two yards is 144 cubits. A cubit, the biblical measurement, is approximately eighteen inches or a foot and a half. This is the distance between the elbow and the tip of the middle finger. Therefore, 144 cubits times eighteen inches is 216 feet or seventy-two yards. Seventy-two yards is approximately three-fourths the length of a football field.

When I saw the New Jerusalem in Eternity, I know the height of the walls was greater than seventy-two yards tall, which is three-fourths of the length of a football field, so this has to be the thickness of the wall.

Seventy-two yards is the width or the thickness of the wall. The King James Bible says it is the width of the wall in its footnotes. If this is how thick the wall is, then there is no scripture that tells us how high or tall the wall is. Only how high the city is, 1,500 miles, and the length of the wall, 1,500 miles.

The massive size of the thickness of the walls not only implies strength but also shows the enormous scale of the city.

The Gates in the Walls

"The New Jerusalem has a great and high wall, with twelve gates and at the gates, twelve angels stationed at each gate and names were written on the gates, which are those of the twelve tribes of Israel" (Revelation 21:12). "And the twelve gates are twelve pearls; each one of the gates is a single pearl" (Revelation 21:21). The pearl has great significance because the pearl was esteemed the greatest value among the ancients and is the only precious stone that man cannot improve.

The city's gates in the walls will never be closed. In ancient cities, their gates would be closed at night for security purposes. However, since there will be no night on the new earth, and all evil has been put down, there are no enemies to close the gates against. The New Jerusalem will have eternal safety and peace, and the gates will always be open.

On each gate is written the name of one of the twelve tribes of Israel. There are three gates on each side of the four walls. The three gates on the east wall, are the names of Joseph, Benjamin, and Dan. On the north gates are Reuben, Judah, and Levi; on the south gates are Simeon, Issachar, and Zebulun; on the west gates are Gad, Asher, and Naphtali (Ezekiel 48:31-34).

The Old Testament is represented in the gates of New Jerusalem by having the name of one of the tribes of Israel on each gate.

The Foundation Stones of the Wall Around the City

"And the wall of the city had twelve foundation stones, and on them were the twelve names of the twelve apostles of the Lamb" (Revelation 21:14). The Bible does not tell us which layer of color represents which apostle.

The New Testament is represented in the layers in the walls of New Jerusalem by having an apostle's name on each layer. The Old Testament is represented in the gates by having the name of one of the tribes of Israel on each gate. The Old Testament tribes of Israel and the New Testament Apostles are the foundation on which New Jerusalem is built.

"The material of the wall was jasper, and the city was pure gold like clear glass" (Revelation 21:18). The Greek states it is bathed in God's light. Revelation 21:19 starts by describing the foundation stones of the wall. "They were adorned with every kind of precious stone. The first foundation stone is jasper; the second is sapphire, the third is chalcedony, the fourth is emerald, the fifth is sardonyx, the sixth is sardius, the seventh is chrysolite, the eighth is beryl, the ninth is topaz, the tenth chrysoprase, the eleventh jacinth, and the twelfth amethyst."

Notice that Revelation 21:18 states that the wall is jasper. In Revelation 21:19, the first foundation stone is jasper, and jasper is also a symbol of strength. When I saw the walls of the New Jerusalem in Eternity, I described the color of the wall above the colored layers as going from a light tan color and getting lighter until the wall reached the top. This scripture says this is the color of Jasper.

The exact composition of these precious stones is not known. The stones are designed to reflect the glory of God in a spectrum of brilliance. The light of the city, which is God's glory, will be shining through these various colors of the twelve foundation layers in the wall.

In the description of the foundation layers, we find jasper, carnelian, and emerald. In Revelation 4:3, these stones have a special significance of glory and majesty that are characteristic of God on His throne. "And He who was sitting was like a jasper stone and a sardius in appearance; and there was a rainbow around the throne, like an emerald in appearance." Jasper might refer to the purity and strength of God. Sardius or carnelian, beautiful blood red like a ruby of God's redemptive purpose and emerald green. John compared the emerald to the rainbow around God's throne of everlasting love. God has a reason and purpose for every color He uses.

The Holy City, New Jerusalem

John tells us he saw four things in Revelation 21:1: "I saw a <u>New Heaven</u> and a <u>New Earth</u> and the <u>first earth passed away</u>, and there is <u>no longer any sea.</u>

The word *sea* could have two different meanings. There is no longer any *sea*, which could simply imply salt water, because God destroyed the earth, and there will be fresh living water flowing in the New Jerusalem. Or sea could mean evil. There will no longer be any evil on the new earth. In John's time, the people believed the sea was evil because when people went out to sea, they did not always return.

The evil nuance of the sea could metaphorically represent the afflictions that threatened God's people in the old world. In John's mind, in the Book of Revelation, he would have seen the tribulations resulting from oppression and sin by the ungodly world. John could have been referring to evil. No longer any sea could mean 1. no water of the sea or 2. there will be no evil. Either way, we know there will be no sea in the New Heaven and on the New Earth.

Remember from our study that New Jerusalem is the Bride, the Wife of Christ. The Saints *will become the Wife of Christ when they start living in New Jerusalem.* One of the seven angels spoke with John saying to him. "Come here, I, the angel, shall show you John, *the bride, the wife* of the Lamb, and the angel carried John away in the Spirit to a great and high mountain and *showed John the holy city, Jerusalem,* coming down out of heaven from God" (Revelation 21:9-10).

The angel showed Apostle John the Bride, the Wife of Jesus. It is the *Holy City, the New Jerusalem,* in the New Heavens, on the New Earth in our Eternity. The angel says the New Jerusalem *is the Bride,* the *Wife of Christ,* and the *Bride, the Wife of Christ,* will live in the New Jerusalem (Revelation 21:9-10). These two scriptures tell us, *"the great city, the Holy Jerusalem, is the Bride, the Wife of Christ."*

The next scriptures tell us who will live in New Jerusalem.

1. The Old Testament Saints were promised to live in New Jerusalem (Hebrew 11:10).
2. The early church and the disciples were promised the city when Jesus told the disciples that He would prepare a place for them in His Father's house (John 14:1-3; Hebrews 13:14).
3. Every born-again Christian believer is promised the city (Revelation 3:12; Hebrews 12:23).
4. The 144,000 Jewish Witnesses and the Two Prophets will be there (Revelation 7:1-8; 12:5; 14:1-5).
5. The Tribulation Saints will be there (Revelation 6:9-11; 7:9- 17; 20:4-6).

The Holy City is a fitting description of the New Jerusalem because the Holy presence of God will abide there forever. Other names for the Holy City are The New Jerusalem, the Bride, the Wife of the Lamb, the Tabernacle of God, the Holy Jerusalem, and the Heavenly Jerusalem. The believers from the Old Testament, the Church, those saved during the Tribulation, and all the believers from the Millennium will be in New Jerusalem.

The Holy City, the New Jerusalem, in Eternity, was designed and built by God. In Revelation 21, John saw the Holy City. Its *name* is the New Jerusalem, and its *origin* is coming down from out of Heaven. Jesus and God are the temple, and it is prepared as the Bride, the Wife of Jesus. The city will be adorned with beauty, and its eternal location is in the New Heaven and on the New Earth.

Revelation 21:10 explains where the New Jerusalem is. "It descends out of heaven from God." In Greek, "out of" means the origin of something, the place where something comes from. The New Jerusalem will set on the New Earth. The New Jerusalem is built on a foundation prepared to set on the earth.

Hebrews 11:10 tells us, "For he (Abraham) was looking for the city which has foundations, whose architect and builder is God." Hebrews 11:16 states that the patriarchs were looking for a better place, a heavenly homeland, and God prepared a city for them. "They desire a better country, that is a heavenly one. God is not ashamed to be called their God; for He has prepared a city for them."

Revelation 21:2-3, "And I, John, saw the holy city, New Jerusalem, coming out of heaven from God, made ready as a bride beautifully dressed for her husband. I heard a loud voice from the throne, saying, Look, the tabernacle of God is among His people, and He will live with them, and they will be His people, and God himself will be with them." God calls us His people, and we will live with Him forever.

The Tree of Life

Starting in Revelation 21:24, the scriptures are giving us more information about the nations. We learned about the nations in our Millennium study. The nations are the earthly people that survived the Tribulation and entered the Millennium. They are in their natural earthly bodies. The question is, what happens to the believing nations at the end of the Millennium?

Revelation 21:24 (NKJ): "And the nations of them which are saved shall walk in the light of it (New Jerusalem), and the kings of the earth do bring their glory and honor into it."

Revelation 21:24 (NAS): "And the nations shall walk by its light, and the kings of the earth shall bring their glory into it (New Jerusalem)."

In Greek "light" is phos from pháo. In this scripture, "light" means to shine, the dazzling light, splendor, or glory which surrounds the throne of God in which He dwells.

Let us break this scripture down.

1. And the nations of them: The natural people in their earthy bodies who lived from the Tribulation period through to the end of the Millennium and are believers.

2. Which are saved: All men on the New Earth will be saved from sin and be righteous eternally. The camp of the Saints in the Millennium will remain (Revelation 20:7-10).

3. Shall walk in the light of it: "It" is the New Jerusalem, and means to shine, the dazzling light, splendor, or glory which surrounds the throne of God in which He dwells.

4. The kings of the earth do bring their glory and honor into it: All the nations will traffic in and bring their glory into the city forever (Revelation 21:24-26).

5. Enter, bring, traffic: they may have the right to the tree of life and may enter in through the gates into the city.

This scripture states that all nations will be saved, and they will walk in accordance with God's will, and they will bring their glory and their honor into the city, New Jerusalem forever.

The nations that were believers and alive at the end of the Millennium will enter Eternity. Their bodies will be changed into an eternal state by God. In Revelation 21:5, God Who sets upon the throne said, "Behold, I am making all things new."

Let us continue with the scriptures on the nations.

Revelation 21:25 (NKJ) explains, "The gates of it (New Jerusalem) shall not be shut at all by day; for there shall be no night there (New Jerusalem). 1. No Night there: This refers to no night in the city, but outside the city, there will be day and night eternally (Psalm 89:2-3; Psalm 89:29-37; Jeremiah 31:35-36).

Revelation 21:26 (NKJ) "And they (the nations) shall bring the glory and honor of the nations into it." The scripture states again, as in Revelation 21:24, that the nations will bring their glory and honor into New Jerusalem.

Revelation 21:27 (NKJ) "And there shall in no wise enter into it anything that defiles (in an evil state), neither whatsoever worketh abomination nor makes a lie, but they which are written in the Lamb's book of life." This is saying that all the nations on the New Earth will be saved and have their names written in the Book of Life. (Revelation 21:24-27).

The nations will carry out the original program that God had for Adam and Eve before the fall. The Tree of Life symbolized Eternal Life in the Garden of Eden and now in New Jerusalem in Eternity.

The tree of life was in the center of the garden of Eden (Genesis 2:9; 3:3). After the fall of mankind into sin, God denied humanity access to the tree (Genesis 3:24). Ezekiel 47:12 speaks of trees that bear fruit with medicinal value. It pictures the New Jerusalem as the new and permanent "Eden," where there shall be no more curse (Genesis 3:14-19). Adam and Eve walked with the Lord periodically in the garden. In New Jerusalem, His presence will be constant.

The Tree of Life in Eternity is for the nations. Revelation 22:1-2 states, "The water of life clear as crystal, coming from the throne of God and of the Lamb in the middle of the street. And on either side of the river was the tree of life, bearing twelve kinds of fruit, yielding its fruit every month (this tells us there is time in Eternity), and the leaves of the tree were for the healing of the nations." The Greek word for healing is theraplah, to heal or to promote health.

This is the preservation of life for the natural nations. Eternal health and life will come from the leaves of the trees. At each of the twelve gates or entrances into New Jerusalem, there will be a great river flowing through the streets, and there will be rows of trees on each side, and the leaves are for eternal health.

Revelation 22:3 states, "And there shall be no more curse, but the throne of God and of the Lamb shall be in it and His servants shall serve Him." The curse is what Satan and Adam brought upon the earth with the fall of man. God's servants will be the faithful redeemed believers, faithful angels, and all others that have not rebelled or have been redeemed from all possibility of rebellion in all Eternity.

Revelation 22:4: "And they (nations) shall see His face and His name shall be in their foreheads." All those in the eternal state will actually look upon God's face, and His name will be in their foreheads. I believe God's name on their forehead is to proclaim that the believers of the Millennial nations belong to God, just as God did with the 144,000 in the Tribulation. He put His name on the foreheads of the 144,000 to show they were His. I believe the nations will live outside of the New Jerusalem on the

New Earth, and they will enter New Jerusalem through the open gates. After learning about the nations, let's go back to New Jerusalem for us,

the Saints that will be living in New Jerusalem. "The water of life clear as crystal, coming from the throne of God and of the Lamb." In the opening words of Revelation 22:1, the angel shows John a river of the water of life, clear as crystal, coming from the throne of God and of the Lamb in the middle of the street. These descriptive words indicate the fullness of life and continuous blessing in New Jerusalem. The river is for the outflow of spiritual benefits. The streets of the city are pure gold, and they are like transparent glass.

There will be no more mourning, crying, pain or sorrow, death or sin. By the time of Eternity, God will have erased all remembrance of the old world (Revelation 21:3).

The Apostle John lists several things that will not be in Eternity. There will be no:

1. temple
2. sun
3. moon
4. night
5. sea
6. curse
7. crying
8. sickness
9. suffering
10. pain
11. mourning
12. sorrow
13. sin
14. death

This is undoubtedly a New Heaven on a New Earth. Praise God!

The Bible does not tell us in any one scripture a complete description of God's plan for our activities during our eternal life. Listed are a few scriptures that give us an idea of what takes place in Eternity.

1. We will see the spiritual appearance of God face to face (Revelation 22:4).

2. We will know believers who existed before us, including the Apostles, Moses, and Abraham (Hebrew 11:10-16).

3. Rest: "They may rest from their labors, for their deeds do follow them" (Revelation 14:13).

4. Knowledge: "Then shall I know even as also I am known" (1 Corinthians 13:12).

5. Joy: "He shall wipe all tears away, no more death, pain, sorrow, or crying" (Revelation 21:4).

6. Service: "The throne of God and the Lamb shall be in it, and His servants shall serve Him" (Revelation 22:3).

7. Abundance: "I will freely give him that thirst of the fountain of the water of life" (Revelation 21:6).

8. Worship: "Hallelujah, Salvation, glory and honor, and power unto the Lord our God" (Revelation 19:1).

The Afterlife Summary

What we will experience in our Afterlife is based on scripture, my study of the Book of Revelation, and the Book of Daniel. My study of the Rapture, the Tribulation, the Millennium, and my time in Eternity.

As believers, we will experience death on this earth, or we will be taken up in the Rapture. We will be transformed from our earthly bodies into glorified resurrected bodies that will last forever, just like Jesus has. We will receive our rewards and crowns in Heaven, and we will experience the most beautiful praise and worship we have ever known. Our time in Heaven will be full of blessings. We are the Bride of Christ, and we will be preparing to attend the banquet, the marriage supper of the Lamb. There will be peace and love beyond what we can possibly imagine. We will return to earth from Heaven with Jesus at His Second Coming.

We will live with Jesus in His Millennial Kingdom for one-thousand-years. We will rule and reign with Jesus over the natural people, the nations. We will enter our eternal home when Jesus delivers us up pure and Holy to be with God in His Holy Kingdom. We will see God face to face, and He will dwell with and among us. We serve a loving God who wants us to be with Him forever.

I call the Book of Revelation a love story because God does everything possible to get our attention and for each one of us to have salvation and eternal life with Him. He pursues us because we are His children, and He loves us.

I pray this book gives you hope and knowledge, and that some of your questions have been answered. I want you to have a deeper understanding of what is ahead of us in our Afterlife.

What I saw in Eternity is beautiful, and is confirmed by the Word of God. I have seen the eternal New Jerusalem. I want you to be looking forward to seeing and living in what is next after our life on this earth is completed. I want you to be anticipating the Rapture and your future in Heaven, the Millennial Kingdom and in Eternity. The magnificent place of New Jerusalem, the New Heaven and on a New Earth prepared for our everlasting eternal life with our Heavenly Father.

GLOSSARY

Abomination: is described as idolatrous worship, indecency, and immorality. Something that causes disgust and is detestable to God and His people.

Desolation: is to destroy, devastate, and leave something in a horrible condition, desecrating or violating something sacred. The Abomination of Desolation of the Holy Temple is a foul and abhorrent thing that will horribly destroy and violate the sacred temple in the middle of the Tribulation.

Eternal: infinite time, duration without end, lasting or existing forever.
Glorified: means to be transformed from our earthly body into a mortal non-decaying body that can live forever in our eternal life. To make the saints whole in body, soul, and spirit to the glory fitted of Christ. This is the same glorified body that Jesus has in Heaven.

Glory of God: means the manifestation of God's presence and seeing the beauty of His Spirit.

Hades: is the New Testament Greek word for Hell and means unseen. Sheol, Hades, and Hell are the same place and in the same place. Luke 16:19-31 describes this place as a realm, an abode, a domain, and a place of activity. The dwelling place beneath the earth for the unredeemed dead or the spirits of the damned. The sinners, the unbelievers, are still in Hades/Hell today.

Holy Spirit: the Holy Spirit is often referred to as the Spirit, the Holy Spirit, the Spirit of God, the Holy Ghost, the Spirit of the Lord, and the Comforter.

Incorruptible: the body is not subject to death and will never decay.

Imperishable: the body cannot be destroyed and is everlasting.

Rapture: is when Jesus takes the Saints to Heaven to be with Him. Rapture comes from the Greek word harpaso, meaning to snatch up suddenly, to be caught up, to carry off.

Redeemed: means to be saved or delivered from sin and its consequences. We were purchased or redeemed by Jesus when He died on the cross. Resurrected, restored, and eternal bodies that will live forever.

Resurrection: means uniting the dead with their soul and spirit. To restore death to life.

Soul: Hebrew word is nephesh. People are a nephesh, a living, breathing, physical being. Nephesh is the whole body, the entire being.

Sanctify: is to set apart for holy service, or more basically, to be made holy. God's purpose for Israel from the start was to set them apart from other peoples by giving them His laws and His statutes.

ACKNOWLEDGMENTS

I want to thank some very special people that have
enriched my life.

First to my husband, daughters, sons in-law, and grandsons
for their unconditional love and support. They are my life
and blessing.

To Pastor Jimmy Evans
Former Pastor of Trinity Fellowship Church Founder and
President of XO Marriage and The Tipping Point
My pastor, teacher, and friend for over thirty-five years

To Pastors Jimmy and Kim Witcher Pastors of Trinity
Fellowship Church
My pastors and teachers, you encourage and cover me

To Pastors John and Carolyn Davis, and Pastors Kyle and
Rita Wilkinson
My prayer partners

www.ingramcontent.com/pod-product-compliance
Lightning Source LLC
Chambersburg PA
CBHW051201120626
46547CB00012B/1154